# Eliminating Satan and Hell

# Eliminating
# SATAN and HELL

Affirming a Compassionate Creator-God

By
V. DONALD EMMEL

WIPF & STOCK · Eugene, Oregon

ELIMINATING SATAN AND HELL
Affirming a Compassionate Creator-God

Copyright © 2013 V. Donald Emmel. All rights reserved. Except for brief quotations in critical publications or reviews, no part of this book may be reproduced in any manner without prior written permission from the publisher. Write: Permissions. Wipf and Stock Publishers, 199 W. 8th Ave., Suite 3, Eugene, OR 97401.

All biblical quotations are from The New Oxford Annotated Bible *New Revised Standard Version Study Bible*. New York: Oxford University Press, 1991.

Wipf & Stock
An Imprint of Wipf and Stock Publishers
199 W. 8th Ave., Suite 3
Eugene, OR 97401

www.wipfandstock.com

ISBN 13: 978-1-62564-411-4

Manufactured in the U.S.A.

# Contents

*Preface* | vii

1. The Basics of Myth and Scriptural Formation | 1
2. Life and Death in Ancient Myths | 9
3. An Alternative Hebrew Community | 17
4. Hebrew Myths of Systemic Evil | 24
5. Hebrew Myths of Life, Death, and Sheol | 31
6. Yahweh: Punitive or Compassionate? | 36
7. Israel, a Monarchy or Servant? | 46
8. Persian Myths and the Introduction of Satan | 55
9. The Cradle for Apocalyptic Myths | 68
10. Greek Myths of Tartarus and Hades | 78
11. Search for a Different Understanding | 84
12. Jewish Apocalyptic Myths | 92
13. Daniel and the Oral Law | 105
14. Jewish Sectarian Groups | 109
15. First-Century Political Conflict | 120
16. Paul on Satan, Sin, Hell, and Related Concepts | 131
17. Satan in the Gospels | 142
18. Hell in the Gospels | 153
19. The Nature of the Creator-God | 162
20. An Unsettled Christendom | 166
21. Postscript | 178

*Bibliography* | 183

# Preface

I BEGAN THIS TOPIC with a bit of anxiety because I am treading on ground that many Christians will call "heretical." The concepts of Satan and Hell have been around for over two thousand years and are ingrained in Roman Catholic, Protestant Evangelical, and Islamic theology. I have struggled with these concepts and have been leery to use the terms. I know there are millions of people who have been taught the doctrines and fear the concepts are correct. I also know there are millions of others who do not believe in the doctrines and hope the concepts are wrong. Recently, I have questioned them more urgently from two personal experiences, a wedding and a Doomsday painting.

The first experience comes from conducting a wedding in 2005 between a Lutheran groom and a Hindu bride. During the wedding I conducted a traditional Christian service. This was followed by a Hindu priestess conducting a traditional Hindu service. Having spent considerable time in premarital counseling with the couple, I came to have a very high regard for the bride and groom. The bride was a Harvard graduate and a vice president of a major Silicon Valley high-tech company. She was a beautiful human being in every way. Could I believe that just because she did not accept Jesus Christ as her Lord that she is lost and condemned to eternal punishment in the fires of Hell? I found myself crying out, "No!" Yet, this is what much Christian dogma asserts. For me this contradicted the gracious, loving, forgiving God that I, as a Presbyterian university pastor and parish pastor, have understood for years from the Judeo-Christian Scriptures. It was then that I began the historical research for this book.

The second experience comes from remembering a Doomsday painting in the St. Thomas Church of Salisbury, England, that my wife and I had the privilege of seeing. The building was constructed around 1200 CE

*Preface*

and dedicated to St. Thomas Beckett. The Doomsday painting above the chancel arch was by far the most striking feature of the church. In the painting Jesus appears dominantly in its center and seated on a rainbow. The Twelve Apostles, in line at his feet, are judging the twelve tribes of Israel. On his right is the Virgin Mary and on his left is John the Baptist. In the background was the New Jerusalem with the faithful crowding its walls.

As one looks at the picture one sees the dead rising from their graves, assisted by angels who are taking the sinless upward into the kingdom of Heaven. Whereas the sinful are handed over to the Prince of Darkness who stands with one foot projecting out of the picture. Around him are the infernal regions where demons are dragging the damned downwards to Hell, represented by the gaping mouth of a monstrous dragon.

The whole scene is clearly designed to emphasize the terrors of Satan and Hell. They warned medieval minds, and perhaps our own, that in God's final judgment there is no respecter of persons. Even the bishop and crowned heads of government were among the condemned. The motto at the bottom read *Nulla est Redemptio*, which literally means "There is no redemption."

Does the Judeo-Christian faith demand a Satan, a hellish punishment for the "unrighteous" and a heavenly reward for the "righteous" in order to make life explainable? Over the centuries these terms have been used to frighten people and condemn others as heretical. In certain religious circles these designations have come to be seen as factual realities and official dogma. But are they simply ancient myths that once gave an understanding about life, but are no longer valid? What if this whole Hell-Satan cosmology is biblically unsupportable and should never have been allowed to infect Judeo-Christian theology?

Underneath these surface questions are deeper questions. If the Creator-God is all-powerful and all good, must you explain evil with a Satan and a Hell? Is this Creator-God wrathful or loving and compassionate? These are questions that have perplexed theologians and philosophers for centuries. This study is written to look at the origin and history of the terms of Hell and Satan, how they have been used, and to challenge their validity as realities for our times. Ultimately this study is about systems of evil that I will often call "systemic evil" and the nature of the Creator-God.

I have often thought of Rousseau's comment in his *Social Contract*: "It is impossible to live in peace with those whom we believe to be damned. To love them would be to hate God who punishes them. It is essential that they either be converted or punished."[1]

"Whom we believed to be damned"? Upon what moral basis do we decide who God punishes? Do we see only a certain segment of Christians as being loved by God and all other people as inferior, lost, or controlled by Satan and thus necessarily condemned to eternal punishment? We will see this dominant theme of human vengeance identified by Rousseau in pagan myths, in Plato, and in apocalyptic literature that it is either the conversion of those with whom we disagree and who are different, or punishment and destruction. But maybe this Creator-God really does love others besides just certain types of Christians.

So I began this journey of research. First, to look at what is in ancient mythologies and in the early Hebrew Scriptures. Second, to look at the sociopolitical conditions between 538 BCE and 60 BCE which gave rise to non-canonical apocalyptic literature wherein we begin to find Satan used as an opponent of God, and Hell as a place to consign sinners. Third, to examine the devastating sociopolitical conditions of both the pre-Christian and early Christian centuries. We must understand the conditions that gave rise of Jewish apocalyptic literature and Christian literature coming out of those periods. Fourth, to look at the first few Christian centuries when the church was separating itself from Judaism and defining what was orthodox and what was heretical, what was of Satan and what was to be condemned to Hell. Finally, to ask myself if there are more accurate ways of identifying, understanding, and dealing with the presence of evil than by using these terms with their threatening contemporary imagery?

In focusing on this project I found I needed to begin with three basic premises. First, I needed to allow that what I may have thought the Hebrew and early Christian texts said might not be what they were really stating. Digging into the extensive literature of this project opened new doors of insight that have had a major impact on my conclusions. Second, I needed to be alive to the vast intellectual and scientific difference between what the mental knapsacks of the ancients contained two thousand years ago, and what ours now contain. Creation is part of our given. Crucial is the information about the age of our universe, the evolution of species and the nature of DNA. I needed to recognize and honor the many questions scientists are raising and respect their scholarship. My conclusions must not fly in the face of what we now know about our humanity and our universe.

1. Rousseau, *Social Contract*, chapter 8.

*Preface*

Third, in many ways I am treading ground regarding mythology that the Marburg theologian Rudolph Bultmann broke open in his *Jesus Christ and Mythology*, published in 1958.

Therefore, I want to respect and use the best current scholarship and literature available in examining the myths and yet write in a way the common person can follow and understand. I recognize that some readers will be familiar with the history and texts I will be covering, but most will not. I want to give sufficient historical background and detail to carry everyone along.

Again, the ultimate question for our study is the differentiation between a cranky, punitive Creator-God doing battle with a Satan and sending to an eternal Hell all who disappoint God. Or, a God who is truly monotheistic and far more compassionate, forgiving, and providing than we can ever imagine. I'll do my best to share the journey of my research.

At first I thought this task would be simple. It was not! I have struggled harder with biblical and nonbiblical writings and raised more questions within myself than any time in my career. I owe major debts of gratitude to those who have encouraged me not to abandon the project. First, to Dr. Herman Waetjen, author and retired New Testament professor at the San Francisco Theological Seminary, a friend and mentor who has persistently challenged me to "keep digging" and not become too encyclopedic! His scholarship and insights have been invaluable. Second, to Jack Batson, a historian and teacher, and the Reverend Jonathan Eastman, a fellow pastor, both of whom have read through the manuscript offering many encouraging suggestions and critical editing. Finally, to my gracious wife, Esther, for her endless patience when more times than one wants to mention saw me staring out the window knowing that I was boxing with the myths of Satan and Hell again. With good humor and love, she put up with a great deal and was always positive about my goal for this book and helped make many corrections.

# 1

# The Basics of Myth and Scriptural Formation

## WEEDS IN THE GARDEN

THERE ARE WEEDS IN all gardens that no longer belong and need pulling out according to Eric Liu and Nick Hanauer in their recent book, *The Gardens of Democracy*. This applies as well to ancient myths. We no longer live in the days of 2500 BCE, or even 500 BCE, when ancient myth-makers developed their stories, trying to explain their pre-scientific universe as best they could with extremely limited knowledge. They developed myths of gods, with evil beings fighting not only each other but also humans, and underground storehouses to punish the evil dead. For the ancients these explained their world. Their personal lives and societies were based upon these myths. They only knew that the sun, moon and stars crossed the skies immediately above them. They did not know our universe extends millions of light-years out into the expanse of the skies. They had no conception of millions of evolutionary years for humans to develop and survive on this planet to become what we now are. They had no biological science telling them about DNA and what can or cannot be inherited. They had stories of an ideal human beginning in a garden where there was no hard work, no pain in childbirth, no death.

The naturalist Edward O. Wilson reminds us in his research on species evolution that ancient societies needed stories to help them understand and explain the meaning of their lives. "The best, the only way our forebears could manage to explain existence itself was a creation myth. And every creation myth, without exception, affirmed the superiority of the tribe that invented it over all other tribes. That much assumed, every religious believer saw himself as a chosen person. Organized religions and their gods, although conceived in ignorance of most of the real world, were unfortunately set in stone in early history."[1]

In this work we must challenge the myths in the garden that no longer work and replace them with the best knowledge we now possess. Our conclusions about hell and Satan must not conflict with the basic science that we know today.

## THE NATURE OF MYTHS

For the ancients their myths were not fairy tales or untruths, but their best constructs that gave meaning and power to what they were experiencing. It was their imaginative way of creating a worldview out of the unseen forces of systemic good and evil, of the realities of pain and happiness, of the prosperity and tragedy of their daily lives. Their mythic stories made stabs at understanding and defining the beginning of creation, the origin of evil, the nature of death, concepts of law and justice, of political order and the use of power.

It is important for this study to clarify that these gods were mythical entities with personalized names representing forces of good and evil. They were never physical entities or actual beings in the cosmos. We also need to recognize these ancient myths are not to be taken literally. The British scholar on religion Karen Armstrong warns us of this in her *History of God*.[2] Therefore, my task in this work is to look at the historical situations out of which the myths of hell and Satan developed and to recognize them for what they were: namely myths. This may be unsettling for many Christians, especially for the biblical literalist. It would be insensitive and a mistake summarily to dismiss their concerns without giving the development and purpose of the ancient myths and supportive reasons for a change of understanding. Fortunately, Rob Bell, in his *Love Wins*, has opened the dialogue for Evangelicals.

---

1. Wilson, *Social Conquest*, 291.
2. Armstrong, *History of God*, 5.

## The Basics of Myth and Scriptural Formation

As the ancients developed their legends, they envisioned a supernatural sphere where these mythic gods lived and interacted with humans on earth. We will bump into Marduk, Enlil, Satan, Belial, and Mastemah, each representing aspects of what I will call "systemic evil." These myths were also developed to reflect and justify current political systems. A double purpose operated. First, a society that used vengeance, male domination, and absolute authority could justify their actions by constructing a mythical sphere of gods who used the same vengeance, male domination, and absolute authority. They could then lay the myth on their subjects claiming what is happening on the supernatural level of the gods should be happening on the earthly level. Thus legitimizing their rule. In the next chapter we will see this in one of the earliest myths, the *Enuma Elish* myth.

### WHEN MYTHS NO LONGER WORK

It is also crucial to look at the nature of myths and how they are used. Kenelm Burridge, in *New Heaven, New Earth*, has completed a major study on myths and millennial developments, both historic and modern. He traces the steps through which mythic constructs that once gave meaning to a group are changed and new ones are developed.

First, there is what Burridge calls an awareness of being disenfranchised. By this Burridge means there is a sense of power coming from an understanding of life that gives a feeling of completeness or at-one-ness with the universe. When the existing myth no longer works and the oneness is shattered, an individual consciously or unconsciously feels disenfranchised and left out. This state of being becomes unbearable, and individuals and/or groups reach out to restore completeness in a way that is intelligible and has integrity. They begin a search into their only universe of knowledge and their past tradition to see what might still be relevant. In this exploration, old convictions are constructed into new myths.

The second phase is to test their new myths against the reality they are experiencing. They attempt to see if there is more economic security, more sense of self-worth; they search for some sense of power in control of their lives so they do not simply feel at the mercy of events. Burridge says much of this may be disorganized until a prophet emerges with a new concept which gives a better sense of reality and coherence to life. The prophet, however, must connect with the traditions of the past and reshape them so there is a relationship to a new security and integrity that would give a cohesive understanding of what is being experienced.

The third phase comes when individuals find others who are sharing the same questions and newly found convictions. They begin then to form like-minded communities around their new myths of explanation. We see in Burridge that myths are not static, nor to be locked in, since they represent a group's thinking for a particular time in history. For that time and place, however, the particular myth was very important to the believers. It gave a framework into which the believer could stand with some assurance since others around them believed the same thing. When outdated, the new myths included changed efforts at understanding the forces of nature, of human activity, of measurements of right and wrong, and concepts of death and judgment.

The new myths or understandings then became definitions of reality, both politically and religiously. Wherever a myth is embodied or personalized into the personhood of a god it becomes difficult to challenge. As such, it retains a legitimacy and unquestioned status quo until new happenings or information force a change. It is my conviction that concepts of hell and Satan which may have worked for the past and may have been given a legitimacy of reality in certain religious circles, are no longer valid in the gardens of our contemporary world given what we now know of our universe, how we understand the human being, and our experience of systemic evil.

### FROM BELIEFS TO INERRANCY

Because this work will be focusing largely upon Judeo-Christian stories and history we need to understand the formation of its literature. Coming out of the struggle for the early Christian community to define itself as opposed to other beliefs, there began to develop carefully defined concepts of what was true and authoritative. Unfortunately, this consigned all other beliefs as heresy to be condemned. Much of this condemnation centered around what authority would be given to Scriptures, which was the subject of great debate by the church fathers during the first Christian centuries as we shall see.

Eventually there developed doctrines that all biblical Scripture was authoritative in revealing the nature of God and the universe. These doctrines were hardened into an inerrancy in the European Middle Ages when the newly developing science conflicted with church doctrine. It was then

*The Basics of Myth and Scriptural Formation*

that some theologians said the earth did not circle around the sun in an inerrant path as Copernicus had confirmed, but that the Scriptures themselves were inerrant in all things. Thus, Copernicus was wrong and must be condemned. This began concepts of biblical literalism, and the inerrancy of Scriptures, that are still alive today in many circles and teachings. It is a huge tree in our gardens that must be replaced with current biblical scholarship. It is my thesis that wherever we come out in this journey about hell, Satan and the nature of God, it must correlate to the world in which we now live, not the world of the ancients or the Middle Ages.

## THE PENTATEUCH FORMATION

At the very beginning of this journey we need to recognize what current biblical scholarship is telling us about how the Hebrew and Christian Scriptures were shaped and reshaped. Becoming clear on this now will be of great help when we later examine various biblical sources and their dates.

In the eighth century BCE, ancient Israelite legends began to be drawn together into written form. These earliest stories were not literal histories of documentable events. Rather, they were ways of interpreting the myths and legends of a particular people called Israel whose god was Yahweh. In the first five books of the Hebrew Bible, called the Pentateuch or Torah, major scholars for the last 150-some years have recognized differences in their narrative language. When these differences were sorted out they identified four different streams of writing.

The first stream is called "J" because "Yahweh" (Jehovah in the German) is the mythic term used for god's name. This J stream was written sometime between 922 and 722 BCE. It contains ancient Hebrew myths of understanding their life at that period of history. In J we find the oldest Hebrew creation myth of Genesis chapters 2 and 3. It is in this oldest stream of J where Yahweh is pictured similar to ancient mythic gods. In this creation myth Yahweh walks in the garden like a mortal, but can't find Adam. It is in the J stream where we find the garden of Eden myth, along with the myth of Adam and Eve, who symbolize not the first man and first woman, but generic humanity and life.

We also find in J the Genesis 6 myth of the Watchers, or Nephelim, who come down from heaven and spread evil upon the earth. This is the prelude to the Noah flood story. We will look in detail at this myth in our chapter 4. We also find in J the Tower of Babel myth, the history of Joseph in Egypt, the revelation at Mt. Sinai, and Israel's sojourn in the wilderness. These early narratives of J appear to be composed by an author or authors living in the southern kingdom of Judah and written sometime after the 922 BCE split of the nation into the north and the south but prior to the destruction of the northern kingdom in 721 BCE.

The second stream is called "E" because "Elohim" is consistently used for the name of God. The author appears to have lived in the northern kingdom about the same time as the J stream, but it has a different reflection on Hebrew history. It contains none of the early Hebrew myths as does J. The E story of Joseph in Egypt differs from J. The E stream also includes the story of Isaac's sacrifice and the law codes of Exodus in chapters 21–23. Years later, after the destruction of the northern kingdom in 721 BCE, someone in the remaining southern kingdom of Judah blended the two stories into one, which scholars call J-E.

A third stream is called "D" because it is centered primarily on the book of Deuteronomy and its law code in chapters 12–26. It is viewed as a larger part of history that also includes Joshua, Judges, 1 and 2 Samuel, and 1 and 2 Kings. There is an emphasis on reform and a centralized worship as seen in a reinstatement of Jewish reform under the reign of Josiah in 621 BCE. Thus, it was written during this same historical period. The Deuteronomic writers had confidence that Yahweh would once again restore Israel and a Davidic kingship.

The fourth stream is called "P" because it reflects an even later period when the priests were dominant. This stream was written during or just following the Babylonian exile of 586 to 536 BCE. While in exile, the Jerusalem temple Zadokite priests felt Yahweh had tabernacled with them in Babylon and did not stay in Jerusalem. When the Zadokites returned to Jerusalem in 536 BCE, they claimed to be the legitimate priests of the rebuilt temple with its laws and observances. During this time we see the Levitical laws developed. It was also when 1 and 2 Chronicles, Job, Ezekiel, chapters 1–39 and 40–55 of Isaiah, and other prophets were written.

For our study, it will be crucial to recognize that Genesis chapter 1 comes from the late P stream and was written hundreds of years after Genesis 2–3 and Genesis 6, both of which come from the early J stream. In later Israelite history these streams were interwoven and reedited into the one book we now have. The book of Exodus, for instance, is a combination of sources from J, E, and P.

## NONBIBLICAL WRITINGS

Later, during the Greek occupation period (325–60 BCE), two sets of writings were developed but were not recognized by the Jews as authoritative revelations of Yahweh and never included in the Hebrew canon. These writings included what is called the Apocrypha and the Pseudepigrapha. We will be examining several of these writings in detail, such as *1 Enoch*, *Jubilees*, and the *Sibylline Oracles*, in which Jewish apocalyptic writers developed their cosmology of hell and gave personal names such as Azazel, Mastemah, and Beliar to powerful forces of evil which were opposed to Yahweh.

## PAUL AND THE GOSPEL'S FORMATION

In the New Testament, Paul is our earliest source for the beliefs of the first Christian communities. It is he who wrote letters to young Gentile churches before the destruction of Jerusalem in 70 CE, and before any of the four gospels were written. We will focus on Paul's seven undisputed letters, especially on Romans, since it is viewed as Paul's basic theology.

When we examine the gospels we also need to be aware of their formation. After a century of debate, a consensus of biblical scholars emerged around 1850 CE attributing priority to Mark as being the oldest, written either just before or just after the Roman destruction of Jerusalem in 70 CE. Mark was the primary source for Matthew and Luke, both of which were written around 80 to 85 CE. Matthew in writing to the Jewish community had a separate source of his own which does not show up in Mark or Luke such as his birth narrative and his organizational structure in groupings such as the Beatitudes. Likewise Luke, in writing to the Gentile community, had a separate source of his own such as his birth narrative, the Prodigal Son, the Good Samaritan, and many parables.

There are also places where Matthew and Luke have a common source of teaching which has no parallel in Mark, such as the detailed Temptation scene, the Sermon on the Mount, the Lord's Prayer, etc. Scholars have distilled these distinct teachings and have called them *Quelle* (German for "teaching") or "Q." It is thought the sayings in Q predate Mark. Whether John used any of these three gospels is a matter of differing opinions by scholars, but they agree that John was the last of the gospels written about 90–100 CE.

## Eliminating Satan and Hell

Although the terms Satan and hell do not show up in the Hebrew Scriptures until after 586 BCE, I want to begin in the next chapter with the earliest of ancient myths in order to watch the historical process toward these terms. This includes the *Enuma Elish* myth, the Gilgamesh Epic, and the Code of Hammurabi. So it is to these myths that we turn.

# 2

# Life and Death in Ancient Myths

IN THIS CHAPTER WE focus on three mythic legends: The *Enuma Elish* myth, the Gilgamesh Epic, and the Code of Hammurabi. In these myths we see the gods as part of a mythic heavenly council. Our time frame is 2000 to 1500 BCE.

## THE ENUMA ELISH MYTH

The *Enuma Elish* myth was written as early as the twelfth century BCE, but goes back to the Sumarians during the twenty-first or twenty-second centuries BCE. It will give us clues to an important political order of tyranny by the powerful, of male domination, and of brutality that was found in Mesopotamian and Babylonian cultures. As we shall see, the Hebrews rejected such a political order. This myth comes out of the same Babylonian or Mesopotamian area from which the biblical Abraham emigrated and is one of the earliest myths of humankind. It recounts the struggle of the mythic gods with order and chaos which emerged in the Middle East region of the Tigris and Euphrates rivers. These great rivers originate in the mountains of southeastern Turkey and western Iran (Persia). At certain times each year, as the snow melts in the mountains, the rivers flood violently southward, overflowing the banks in Mesopotamia and destroying villages, farms and homes. The power and chaos they produce is represented in the myth of

*Enuma Elish* by Tiamat, the name for the goddess of chaos. In the myth, order overcomes chaos and was used to justify a then-current political and social order of Babylon.

The myth gives a picture of what must be seen as both a conflicted and chaotic society, but also its top-down social structure. It begins with three primordial gods: Apsu, Mummu, and Tiamat. Apsu was the name for the primary god. Mummu was the name for the adviser to Apsu. Tiamat was the name for the female who gave birth to other gods and was also the goddess of the sea and the goddess of chaos. In the myth, the children of Apsu and Tiamat had banded together and were causing such havoc in the heavens to the point where both Apsu and Tiamat were getting no relief by day or rest by night.

Apsu consulted with his adviser, Mummu, and decided to destroy the bothersome children. But as soon as mother Tiamat heard their plan she rebelled. Mummu's advice to Apsu was to ignore Tiamat and destroy the kids anyway. Ea, the name for one of the wise young gods, saw through Apsu's scheme and killed Apsu. Ea then became the primary god. He married Damkina and to them was born Marduk, named as the most powerful and wisest of all the gods.

Tiamat was still enraged about the threat to her children. Encouraged by the other gods, especially the consort of Tiamat named Kingu, Tiamat gathered her forces and turned against Marduk to destroy him. In the battle Marduk killed Tiamat and split her into two pieces. With half of her he made the sky and with the other half he made the firmament. Thus, the earthly creation in this myth began out of anger, vengeance, and murder which legitimized the anger, vengeance, and murder going on in that society.

Marduk learned it was Kingu who had caused Tiamat to rise against him. So Marduk and Ea bound Kingu and murdered him. Out of Kingu's blood Marduk created humankind to be slaves to serve the gods. Thus, humans were also created out of savagery and to be placed at the bottom of the social structure. In the myth Marduk was proclaimed the supreme god, the one to whom all other gods and humans must bow down and obey. And significantly, human society should replicate what was wrought in the heavens.

In this myth we see all the foundational elements of the Babylonian social structure to establish a dominating order in the midst of power and chaos. The various gods, given names to represent aspects of life, are part of a heavenly court. Marduk is the supreme king who is to be worshiped and obeyed as the supreme god and lord of all. As king, he also has permission to use violence to destroy all threatening opponents including his own mother. We need to be clear that the myth creators had no other analogies by which to describe their gods than the humans they knew. Therefore, their gods were endowed with all the human emotions of ambition and power, love and compassion, hate and revenge. We see the parents' irritation from the kids causing a ruckus; a dad deciding on his own to do the kids in; the anger of mom at such a thought. We see a kid's revengeful killing of dad, a deadly combat between Tiamat and Marduk, and a slaughter of Kingu. The dark sides of daily human life are imbedded into and acted out by the gods.

The social power structure is from Marduk and the elite gods at the top with humans on the bottom as their slaves. In short, the myth builds a two-way social structure: the legitimization of the social structure of the gods, and the legitimization of the powerful kings on earth. The twist comes in humans claiming that what happens on earth is caused by the very gods which humans have created in their myths. Thus the myth works both ways. What is labeled as evil is that which disrupts the harmony and the established power of those at the top as defined by the elite.

Over the centuries, the basics of this myth continue to operate in kingships, dictatorships, corporations, and religious communities where powerful leaders exercise a rule that makes those under them subservient and exploited for the leaders' ends. There is judgment, and a reward is given for those who comply. Damnation and death are for those who get in the way. The elites with their power and money control the legal structures of society and the conditions for all the workers under them. Those in power also determine who are the expendable and damned. Again and again we shall see the Hebrews suffering under this type of social structure. It is crucial that we recognize reward and violence as existing in this mythic construct and throughout ancient societies. It also survives today in many levels of dominance and control in contemporary societies and institutions.

Relevant to our study in this *Enuma Elish* myth, violence and death come into play as the punishment. There is an underworld but there is no concept of hell as a place of eternal punishment. Likewise, there is no concept of a separate personified evil being, a Satan, since the supreme gods such as Marduk, Tiamat exercise goodness as well as vengeance and are all part of a mythic cosmic council.

# Eliminating Satan and Hell

## THE GILGAMESH EPIC

The Gilgamesh Epic is important because it has a flood story with the destruction of the whole earth, which some scholars see as the prototype for the Noah flood myth. This Gilgamesh myth began with stories which Sumerians had written as separate tales. Around 2000 BCE these tales were put together as one poem. Like the *Enuma Elish* myth, this one also originated from the regions of the Tigris and Euphrates rivers and their seasonal floods. At its core it is a mythic legend trying to understand the willfulness of humans against the gods and why people had to die.

Gilgamesh is the hero, born in the city of Uruk. He is two-thirds god and one-third human, and said to be strong and awesome to perfection. Anu is the name of the chief God, and Aruru is the name for his female companion; they are the creators of humankind. Aruru creates Enkidu to be a match in strength for Gilgamesh. Enkidu is a grizzly fellow who lives in the wilds with the animals and is the opposite of Gilgamesh who lives in the city.

In the myth there is a skirmish between Gilgamesh and Enkidu. But instead of becoming bitter antagonists they become close friends. Among the other gods was one named Enlil who assigned Humbaba as a terror to human beings. Humbaba's roar is a Flood, his mouth is Fire, and his breath is Death! Gilgamesh and Enkidu set out to destroy Humbaba thinking that if they murder him there will be rejoicing all over the land. So they proceed to kill Humbaba.

The goddess Ishtar, on seeing the strength and beauty of Gilgamesh, asks him to be her husband. Gilgamesh, however, recites to her the many past lovers she has treated shamefully and rejects her request. Greatly offended, Ishtar goes to Anu, her father, saying, "Father, give me the Bull of Heaven, so he can kill Gilgamesh in his dwelling." Then Ishtar leads the Bull down to earth to kill Gilgamesh and Enkidu. However, Gilgamesh and Enkidu kill the Bull instead. Anu, Enlil, and Shamash then hold a vengeful council and determine that since Gilgamesh and Enkidu have killed the Bull of Heaven, one of them should die. It is Enkidu who dies and Gilgamesh is brokenhearted. Again, we see patterns of anger and vengeance among the gods replicated in ancient Mesopotamian societies.

Gilgamesh now begins his search of the earth for an answer to death. He finds Utnapishtim in the Faraway, across the Waters of Death in the land of the dead at the edge of the earth. He asks Utnapishtim, "Am I not like Enkidu? Will I lie down and never get up again?" In response, Utnapishtim states that death is a natural part of human existence. In our study, it is important to note that death was not seen in this myth as a penalty due to human misdeeds.

Utnapishtim tells Gilgamesh about Enlil, the god of air, storms, and floods, who, because humanity had angered him, sent a great flood to destroy all of humankind. Utnapishtim tells Gilgamesh about building a great boat on which Utnapishtim takes his family and the seed of all the living beings. After many days of rain with the flood covering the earth, Utnapishtim sends out first a dove which returns, then a swallow which returns, neither of which could find a place to land above the waters. He finally sends out a raven which does not return because the waters had receded. The parallel to the later Noah flood myth is obvious.

After the flood, Enlil was furious that the flood had not destroyed humanity and everything else. He was especially angry when Utnapishtim, his family and the seed of every living thing had survived. Nothing was to survive the annihilation. In the character of Enlil we see again a god of hatred, vengeance, and a desire to destroy humanity. There is no indication, except in Enlil's mind, why humanity had become so evil that it needed to be destroyed. Since the mythic Enlil is part of the heavenly pantheon and the dispenser of both good and evil, he can only be partly classified as an antihuman god or representative of evil. Thus, Enlil is not a Satan in our contemporary sense.

Since the gods defined what was evil, they made personal judgments on who and what was good and who and what was wicked and what reward or punishment was to be required. There are no specific laws being followed. Again, death is not a punishment since all things eventually die. But there is a concept that the dead still existed in a location far away from the living, in a place called the House of Darkness and the House of Dust. However, there is no concept of eternal punishment for the wicked and therefore no hell.

## THE CODE OF HAMMURABI

In societies that reflect the *Enuma Elish* myth, good and evil were determined by simple obedience or disobedience to the commands of the ruler. In more advanced ancient societies, however, the social fabric became a system of laws which set the boundaries and measures of human behavior. This was a major step away from the whims of the gods and became especially important as nomadic tribes settled into propertied communities where property rights and trading between communities needed clear definitions.

One of the amazing discoveries of Babylonian history is the Code of Hammurabi coming from a remarkable and wise king, Hammurabi, whose reign dates from 1795 to 1750 BCE. These laws were inscribed on stone tablets standing over eight feet tall and were discovered in Persia in 1901. In this Code we begin to see justice measured by carefully defined law.

This legend begins by acknowledging the Babylonian gods, and we again meet the mythic Marduk, the son of Ea. In the myth, Ea was the god of righteousness who gave Marduk dominion over humankind who then established a great kingdom. We also meet the gods Anu and Bel, who asked Hammurabi, the exalted prince, to create the rule of righteousness for the kingdom. Its purpose was to destroy the wicked and the evildoers so that the strong should not harm the weak.

Here we see the beginning of a systematic separation of the righteous from the wicked, measured by a rule of law for the benefit of humankind. It was Hammurabi who then developed a detailed code of 282 laws to cover all elements of human relationships from contracts and property laws, to irrigation, marriage, divorce, family relations, and violations of many sorts. The following are examples of justice to be measured by law. For instance in rule 2, if anyone brings an accusation against another man, and the accused must go into the river, if he sinks in the river, his accuser shall take possession of his house. But if he survives the river it proves he is not guilty. Then the one who had brought the accusation will be put to death. The one originally accused will then take possession of the house that had belonged to his accuser. In rules 195 to 200 we see if a son strikes his father, his hands shall be cut off; if a man puts out the eye of another man, his eye shall be put out; if he breaks another man's bone, his bone shall be broken; if he puts out the eye of a freed man, or breaks the bone of a freed man, he shall pay one gold mina; if he puts out the eye of a man's slave, or breaks the bone of a man's slave, he shall pay; if a man knocks out the teeth of his equal, his teeth shall be knocked out.

The Babylonians understood evil to be a reality, necessitating the beginning of established law as the criterion for what is good and what is wrong. The rules were precise and the concept of *lex talionis*, an eye for an eye and a tooth for a tooth, operated. The Code was harsh and inflexible upon the guilty. Severe crimes were punished by death. If a new house fell and killed the new owner, the builder was killed. If it also killed the new owner's son, the builder's son was also killed. Even if one testified falsely they were to be killed. In many cases, as we saw in rule 2, the accused person was thrown into the river. Overall, Hammurabi's Code was an advanced paradigm of legal formulations and justice where individuals were singled out and obedience to the law was praised and rewarded; disobedience required judgment and punishment. This was a major step beyond the whims of the gods.

The Code itself is a documented historical reality; there are copies of it. But behind the Code is the myth of Marduk and other gods. In contrast to the *Enuma Elish* myth, the gods here are concerned for justice so that the strong should not harm the weak, to enlighten the land, and to further the well-being of humankind. The gods showed compassion for the weak, and the law was their measure, not the whims of the gods. This is a step forward and may be the first evidence of a society recognizing that laws and regulations were not just for the elite and the powerful.

However, such legalisms have at least four major problems: First, law codes can only measure innocence or guilt. Of itself, the law is not flexible and cannot show mercy. If one is guilty, justice requires there must be a penalty. Second, there is a question of who makes the laws and for whose benefit. The elite and powerful are usually the lawmakers to their own benefit, to the detriment of the rest. Third, one may follow all the laws and still not be caring or loving, and thus may be harmful to others and to creation. Finally, the element of revenge and violent destruction is mixed into all penalties. The one who is sinned against wants to make sure the offender receives due punishment. In the standards of the Hammurabi Code with *lex talionis*, exact punishments are spelled out and take place in this life. The ultimate penalty of death ends everything. We will find this *lex talionis* principle showing up hundreds of years later in the Hebrew Bible, in Exodus 21–22.

With death being the end for everyone, the concept of a hell does not come into play, since hell requires a theory of life after death where one can be eternally punished. There is no personification of evil as a named god and thus no Satan.

## CONCLUSIONS

I have included these early myths for us to see a number of developments:

## Eliminating Satan and Hell

First, the ancients developed myths about the systems of good and evil which they daily experienced. They personalized and humanized these forces as gods with mythic names and in this process it gave their best explanation for what was happening to them. The humans lived on earth; the mythic gods were viewed as living in a supernatural realm. It is very important for us to recognize the gods and their names are figures of speech. They are not real entities.

Second, in the *Enuma Elish* myth we saw a chaotic situation involving a hierarchical society, wherein power was savage, dictatorial, and dehumanizing. This system was ruled by the gods who demanded that humans serve them. It was, however, a system which overcame chaos. This sociopolitical structure, with its elements of violence, was widespread in the Middle East and the ancient Mediterranean world at the human level and continues today. In *Enuma Elish* we saw what was defined as evil was determined by the gods in power. But there was no single personification of a Satan, and death is the end of existence with no afterlife or punishing hell.

Third, the Gilgamesh Epic is important as an early flood story. The society was still hierarchical. There was no rule of law. Enlil was the element of violence and wanted to take vengeance on humanity, but he was only a partial personification of evil. We saw death as where all people die and afterwards are in a place far, far away. Any punishment for evil occurred prior to death, or death itself became the punishment, not in an afterlife hell. There is no Satan.

Fourth, in the *Hammurabi Code* we saw the early development of law as an impersonal measure of behavior. There was more structure and accountability in the rule of law than the rule of the gods. There were designated laws of punishment for the disobedient. The afterlife was nothing more than a shadowy existence in the nether region at the edge of the earth. We saw systemic evil measured by law, but no personification of an evil Satan nor an afterdeath of punishing hell. But we continue to see an element of human revenge in the exercise of law and punishment.

Next, I want to examine the uniqueness of the Hebrew exodus from Egypt and their experience of the Sinai covenant. There we will find a mutual commitment between Yahweh and the people with a defined social structure that is in direct contrast to what we have seen in these three early myths.

# 3

# An Alternative Hebrew Community

THE EARLY MYTHS WE have examined were top-down societies with imperial sovereigns at the top. A major key to understanding Judaism is its contrasting experience with Yahweh in both the exodus from Egypt and the Sinai covenant made between their god and the Hebrew people. The Exodus story was originally told and retold during the early settlement of Israel. Scholars debate when it was finally written down: prior to or during the Davidic monarchy, or even later during the time of the eighth-century prophets. However, as mentioned in our chapter 1, the current book of Exodus is a combination of reediting from J, E, and P by the priests during the much later 587 to 536 BCE Babylonian exile. Thus, it takes the legends and history of Israel and reframes them to speak to a nation whose leadership is in exile and to the people left behind in a destroyed Jerusalem.

## THE EXODUS EXPERIENCE

The understanding of their god, Yahweh, is deeply rooted in this Exodus experience. The story contains mythic language and imagery as did all such writings of ancient history. To begin, we read in Genesis 47 that when a famine had decimated Canaan, some Hebrews fled to Egypt. But when Egypt also experienced a subsequent hard famine, these Hebrews gave all their money to Pharaoh for food. When the food and money were gone they gave all their livestock to Pharaoh. When all that was gone they sold themselves into slavery to Pharaoh. From then on they labored under harsh and unbearable conditions. Like in the *Enuma Elish* myth, the Hebrews suffered under a social structure which saw the Hebrew slaves' primary purpose was to toil and do physical labor so the elite of Egypt might spend their time in leisure.

According to George Mendenhall, University of Michigan professor of Eastern languages, evidence shows that by 1200 BCE there were large concentrations of Hebrew refugees in Egypt.[1] According to legend, Moses had grown up in the Pharaoh's household and thus had hierarchical status. One day he was greatly angered by a guard who beat a fellow Hebrew. Killing the guard, he fled in fear to Midian in the East, joined up with a Midianite priest's family and married one of their daughters. During this time Moses experienced the presence of divinity calling him back to Egypt to lead some slaves through the desert to the land of Canaan and there establish a new kind of human community. When asked this divinity's name, the answer was "I am who I am," the cultic name for the God of Israel, pronounced YHWH or Yahweh (Exod 3:13–14). This Yahweh promised to go with Moses and lead him.

Moses then went back to Egypt and eventually fled into the Sinai wilderness with about seventy families of slaves. The biblical figure of six hundred thousand men is a later erroneous insertion. As Mendenhall has observed, such an exodus group of men, along their with wives and children, would have totaled over two million. Such a group would have been over two hundred miles long![2] Thus began the Hebrews' journey and their conviction that Yahweh had heard their cry, had shown deep compassion, and would lead them out of their oppressive slavery. This conviction was the beginning of a historical trust of Yahweh's commitment to the Hebrews and is seen in all the rest of the writings in the Hebrew canon. We will come back to this again and again.

It is important to recognize Yahweh was not appointing Moses to be another dominating overlord as in the *Enuma Elish* myth or even similar to the Egyptian pharaohs. Exodus tells us that Moses was not a kingly person, but slow of speech and slow of tongue (Exod 4:10). He even pleaded with Yahweh to appoint someone else to leadership (Exod 4:13). But he was

---

1. Mendenhall, *Ancient Israel's Faith*, 44.
2. Ibid., 52.

*An Alternative Hebrew Community*

called to form a new and different type of human community covenanted to Yahweh as their Lord and King.

In the wilderness where there was no water and no food, Yahweh showed compassion and generously provided for them. The Hebrews mumbled and grumbled, but they became a community devoted to Yahweh. At Sinai they learned their Yahweh was not distant nor hostile but graciously walking with them. Yahweh would provide. The Exodus was the Hebrews' liberation to a new world and here they began their attempt to develop a new form of human society based on gratefulness for the goodness of their god, Yahweh.

## THE SINAI COVENANT

At Sinai they were given a new covenant. What has been called the Ten Commandments may be more truthfully called the Ten Commitments. This covenant concept was not something new but took the form of ancient treaties with which the band of slaves were familiar. The commitments were not something uttered by a demanding deity but more accurately are statements and co-commitments of a compassionate god with a tribal band of former slaves. These commitments contain no rules of punishment like the Code of Hammurabi. Mendenhall comments:

> The Decalogue thus provides not a *proscription* against bad conduct but a *description* of a religious value system, in this case, the ethical obligations and personal commitments that provide the foundation of any and all human communities. These obligations are stated not demanded. As in any covenant, the commandments must be voluntarily embraced and undertaken freely and gladly in grateful response for benefits and blessing already received. . . . People must see for themselves that these principles are compelling and good.
> But the Decalogue insists that these religiously grounded commitments are always the primary and essential control mechanisms making any community possible. Unless people possess integrity in these fundamental aspects of life, no community can long endure, regardless of how strong its nationalism, ethnicity, tribal bonds, or social institutions may be. In other words, the Decalogue describes Yahweh's will simply as those ten basic

commitments necessary to maintain human community with a minimum of conflict.[3]

It is crucial to understand that this co-commitment is in sharp contrast to the vengeance and control of the gods in the *Enuma Elish* myth and even different from the rigid laws of the Code of Hammurabi. Yahweh's compassion and mercy was freely offered to this new band of humanity. And this new humanity offered back its gratitude and singular commitment to this gracious Yahweh. "I will be your God. . . . We will be your faithful people." This covenant was a relationship of love, trust, loyalty and service between two entities, the Hebrews and Yahweh. Thus the band of people were changed to be a people with a religious relationship to Yahweh that would be the template for all humanity. United by a spiritual conscience to worship Yahweh and Yahweh alone, Mendenhall states that this allowed the Hebrew tribes to exist for over two centuries without any organized army of force.[4] If anything, the co-commitments are not based on a justice of law, but a justice of compassion and mutual respect by each party.

Years later, the Israelites rationalized that they wanted to become a strong political kingdom to keep at bay incursions from neighboring powers, especially the Philistines who were a constant menace on Israel's southwestern flank. Gideon, one of the judges of Israel, had been successful against many neighboring raids upon them. The people wanted him to become their king. "You rule over us, you and your son and your grandson." Gideon responded, "I will not rule over you, and my son will not rule over you, the Lord will rule over you" (Judg 8:22–23).

Gideon recognized that such traditional kingships always engendered elites who felt they were appointed by the gods to lord over the common people. Kingships would establish an ethical dualism of rulers who claimed a monopoly of divine guidance versus the rest of the population who were seen as lesser, expendable human beings. Laws and regulations would be developed to control the lesser people. The laws would proscribe judgment, and judgment would proscribe punishment which the Sinai covenant did not have. Gideon also rejected the concept of dominant kingship with a son following a father and a grandson following a son. In essence, he reconfirmed the Sinai concept that Yahweh alone would be their king.

Later, ignoring the protests of prophets such as Samuel, and in defiance of Yahweh, the Israelites established kingships under Saul, then David,

3. Ibid., 60–62.
4. Ibid., 80.

and then Solomon. On the one hand, this caused tension from remembering their slavery in Egypt with Yahweh's tender care and their covenanted loyalty to worship Yahweh alone as their King. On the other hand, there were those who sought to replicate a monarchy and a king with all the trappings of armies, coercive laws, and the peoples' loyalties obligated to a human ruler. This was a step away from Yahweh being their King as had been true under the earlier period of the judges. For later Hebrew prophets the concept of human kingship would always be a negative since it was seen as a rejection of Yahweh and the basics of the Sinai covenant. The biblical prophets consistently condemned the kingship arrangement. The prophet Hosea, prior to the fall of the northern kingdom in 721 BCE, had already condemned the concept of kingship (Hos 8:4; 9:15; 10:3, 9). Wise interpreters, such as Ezekiel during the 587 BCE exile, also saw the concept of human kingship as having ended in failure and called for the reestablishment of Yahweh as King (Ezek 20:33).

## COMMUNITY VS. INDIVIDUAL

We also need to recognize in Hebrew covenant theology that it is Yahweh who breathes life into each human being and upon whom each human being is dependent for existence. Thus, the human being does not exist apart from relationship with Yahweh and is also dependent upon community. Each person's identity, then, was bound up as part of a village of probably no more than one hundred to one thousand individuals. The identity of the village was bound as part of the whole nation under Yahweh. Thus, Yahweh's message of justice was not addressed to individuals, but to the whole community which had broken the Sinai covenant relationship. The reciprocal nature of this communal covenant is broadly stated in the reciprocity code of Deuteronomy 30. I will be your God—you will be my people.

> See, I have set before you today life and prosperity, death and adversity. If you obey the commandments of the Lord your God, that I am commanding you today, by loving the Lord your God, walking in his ways, observing the commandments, decrees, and ordinances, then you shall live and become numerous, and the Lord your God will bless you in the land that you are entering. But if your heart turns astray to bend down to others gods and serve them, I declare to you today that you shall perish, and you shall not live long in that land that you are crossing the Jordan to enter and possess. . . . I call heaven and earth to witness against

> you today that I have set before you life and death. Choose life so that you and your descendants may live, loving the Lord your God, obeying him, and holding fast to him; for that means life to you and length of days. (Deut 30:15–20)

But what happens if the people fail their end of this reciprocal relationship? Consistently, the biblical prophets were concerned with their nation's sin as the sin of the whole community. If one person sinned it was the whole of Yahweh's chosen people that was infected. Prior to the Babylonian exile in 587 BCE, the prophet Jeremiah predicted the "people of Judah" will be destroyed as corpses in the Valley of the son of Hinnom (*gehenna*) unless they change directions (Jer 7:30–34). This is Jeremiah's corporate indictment of Judah, not of individuals or certain groups. The whole community was responsible for keeping individuals obedient so as to receive the blessings of Yahweh. If one individual sinned the punishment fell on the whole community. We also see this corporate designation during the exile in Second Isaiah 53 when the whole of Israel is pictured as the Suffering Servant which had sinned and which carried the consequences of its choices.

> Surely he (Israel) has borne our (Israel's) infirmities
> and carried our diseases;
> yet we accounted him stricken,
> struck down by God, and afflicted.
> But he [Israel] was wounded for our transgressions,
> crushed for our iniquities;
> upon him was the punishment that made us whole,
> and by his bruises we are healed.
> All we [Israel] like sheep have gone astray;
> we have all turned to our own way,
> and the LORD has laid on him [Israel]
> the iniquity of us all. (Isa 53:4–6)

When the Israelites understood and interpreted the "acts of god" such as drought, plague and famine as punishments, they saw this as a communal and national punishment. The concepts of individual sin and a revengeful punishment are not yet here.

## CONCLUSIONS

In this chapter we have seen a very important concept of the Hebrews being called to form a new and different style human community centered around gratitude for their god, Yahweh. They experienced Yahweh as a powerful god who heard their cries and was full of goodness and compassion. In the Sinai covenant there is a coequal, voluntary agreement between the people and Yahweh that Israel would be Yahweh's people and Yahweh would be their god. This new community was also equally responsible for each other, including the unfortunate and the poor. This was a rejection of the *Enuma Elish* vertical political structure with the gods at the top and humans as slaves at the bottom serving the gods. It was a rejection of the use of violence by the gods or against each other. There is also no individual judgment and revenge, but rather a communal judgment. In it there is no concept of a personalized Satan or an after-life hell. The Sinai covenant became the standard template for the concept of Yahweh's kingship on earth for future generations of Hebrews.

In the next chapter I want to examine the development of early Hebrew concepts of evil since the myths of Satan and hell are directly related to concepts of evil. This will include asking some hard questions.

# 4

# Hebrew Myths of Systemic Evil

The experience of evil people and actions is found in all cultures. This means evil not just in individuals but in the whole social, economic, and political systems of a society. The struggle for understanding the meaning and origin of what I will be calling "systemic evil" was part of the Hebrew search for truth. We will look first at Genesis chapters 2–3 and Genesis 6 from the J stream of writing (ca. 922 to 722 BCE), and then the much later Genesis chapter 1 from the P stream of writing (ca. 586 to 536 BCE).

## ORIGIN OF EVIL IN GENESIS 2–3

The first and oldest concept of systemic evil in the Bible is in the familiar myth of the fall in Genesis 2–3. There is no indication when this legend was first developed. However, it is clear this is a mythic legend with Hebrew roots reaching back into earlier Near Eastern mythologies with a unique Hebrew interpretation of their god and of human creation. It was certainly written after the 1200 BCE exodus experience. In this creation myth we see the god, Yahweh, pictured as very humanlike, similar to other ancient creations myths. Yahweh had to hunt for Adam in the garden of Eden. The garden of Eden is pictured as an idyllic habitat that provided everything the human beings needed and where there is no strife, no evil, no death.

We know, however, from current science that creation of the universe took place some 13.7 billion years ago. Life itself did not start in an ideal garden with fully constructed human beings but rather over millions of years of evolutionary development. Life has always been a struggle for survival and only the wisest, most cooperative, and strongest survive. Today we know this mythic garden of Eden never actually existed, but the myth helped the Hebrews explain for themselves the beginning of humanity on earth.

The Genesis 2–3 story contains two mythic characters representing humanity. The Hebrew word for Adam represents "humankind." The word for Eve represents "life." The two terms are collective nouns for all of humanity and life. Thus, the story is mythic and not about the first two historic human beings of creation but rather a symbolic recognition that humanity had a beginning. In this myth, Yahweh gives humanity the freedom of choice. It was the mythic snake, part of the creation that Yahweh called "good," that voiced to humans that they have the freedom of standing in opposition to Yahweh. There is no enemy "Satan" in this myth as later misinterpreted.

This Genesis 2–3 Hebrew myth portrays humanity as having been created to be in a communal commitment with Yahweh. This would be a commitment of love, of trust, of obedience, and to be co-stewards of the earth with Yahweh. In essence, this story recaptures the joint commitments we have just seen in the Sinai covenant. In the myth it was pictured that humans sought to escape this relationship and wanted to be like Yahweh, knowing all good and evil. Thus the harmonious relationship was shattered and humanity stood on its own outside the perfect garden. This is the way the Genesis 2–3 writer mythologized it.

## SOME HARD QUESTIONS

It is here where we need to ask some hard questions about the Genesis 2–3 setting as it was first developed orally and finally put into print. What were the Hebrews confronting in real life and history? If the date of the J stream in which this myth is found is correct, then the cultural days of an idealized King David were over. The kingdom had split. The period of bad kings had begun and systemic evil was rampant. The prophets Amos and Hosea were giving sharp warnings about the estranged status of the Hebrew community departing from Yahweh.

Life was still one of hard physical, unending labor of creating a livelihood from the barren, rocky soils of Canaan. Their women faced the pain and dangers of childbirth. Death was a constant reality which cut down some in childhood, others in battle or midlife, and some very late, each one a hard parting. There was no escaping death. When this creation myth was developed it began with the concept of a perfect garden of Eden where none of these hardships existed. In the myth there was no pain, no death, no enemies, and in addition, all was in obedience to the Creator. Since these tough issues were constantly faced, it would be logical for the Hebrews to develop the myth that once in an idealized past these unpleasant conditions did not exist. But in their present life "outside the garden" they began to mythologize hard work, painful childbirth, and death as penalties.

## ARE THESE PENALTIES?

It is here that we today need to challenge later interpretations of this creation myth on at least two points. First, hard work, childbirth, and death are essential realities for continued life on this planet. Without the toil of the earth and its resultant need for food, the human body cannot exist. Without childbirth and its physical pain due to the construction of the female reproductive system, there is no further human creation. Without the death of all creation, including all animals and plants, overcrowding on our planet would soon make life impossible. These representations of hard work, pain in childbirth, and death as penalties worked for this early myth. Today we know these are not penalties from an angry god, but simply the essential realities of all life. This part of the myth is no longer viable as a rational, scientific explanation.

Second, freedom of choice is essential for there to be human history. The Hebrew understanding of history is of an ideal garden of Eden at the beginning of history and a return to an Eden-like existence at the end of history. If the beginning Eden and the end Eden were never separated there would have been no human history. This God-allowed freedom of human choice is what has allowed human history to evolve. In this Hebrew understanding, the freedom of choosing between right or wrong is a basic factor of Yahweh's creation. It is Yahweh who gave humanity the freedom to say "yes" or "no." Yes, they proclaimed that Yahweh gave them the freedom to rebel and to choose evil. Humans were not created to be puppets.

Next we must examine the meaning of "Adam" and "Eve." When one looks carefully in the Hebrew canon it is significant that, apart from this creation myth in Genesis 2–3, "Adam" as a name is used in only one other place, namely in 1 Chronicles 1:1, where it is in a *genealogical list* of

## Hebrew Myths of Systemic Evil

names. "Adam" shows up twice as *geographical locations*: namely in Joshua 3:16 where Adam is ". . . the city that is beside Zarethan," and in Hosea 6:6 where it is also a location. ". . . at Adam they transgressed the covenant." Peter Enns is a senior fellow of biblical studies for the BioLogos Foundation, which explores the integration of science and the Christian faith. He reminds us that there is no indication that Adam's disobedience caused universal human sin or death and there is no further mention of Adam's act in the Hebrew canon.[1]

It is important to recognize that in Genesis, "Adam" is a representative term for humanity, not the first human. Keeping this in mind will help greatly when we look at how Paul used Adam. The term "Eve" is never used again in the Hebrew biblical writings. The concept of the "garden of Eden" does show up in Isaiah 51:3, Joel 2:3, and in several places in Ezekiel chapters 27, 28, and 31, but always as a symbol of the perfect place to which God will restore Zion. Thus, these three terms, Adam, Eve, the garden of Eden, were not ones on which later Hebrew theology was built. For the most part, when the Hebrews looked for an ideal relationship between humanity and Yahweh it was always back to the template of the Sinai covenant's co-commitments.

In Genesis 2–3 the responsibility of evil is kept squarely upon human shoulders and is a result of the choices of humanity. It is not from a celestial satanic being fighting against Yahweh as in our concepts of Satan today. However, this myth recognized that something was amiss, that systemic evil was very much part of the human experience.

## ORIGIN OF EVIL IN GENESIS 6

However, there is a second mythic understanding of how systemic evil entered into the stream of humanity in Genesis 6.

> When people began to multiply on the face of the ground, and daughters were born to them, the sons of God saw that they were fair; and they took wives for themselves of all that they chose. Then the Lord said, "My spirit shall not abide in mortals forever, for they are flesh; their days shall be one hundred and twenty years." The Nephilim were on the earth in those days—and also afterwards—when the sons of God went in to the daughters of humans, who bore children to them. These were the heroes that

---

1. Enns, *Evolution of Adam*, 82.

were of old, warriors of renown. The Lord saw that the wickedness of humankind was great in the earth, and that every inclination of the thoughts of their hearts was only evil continually. And the Lord was sorry that he had made humankind on the earth, and it grieved him to his heart. So the Lord said, "I will blot out from the earth the human beings I have created—people together with animals and creeping things and birds of the air, for I am sorry that I have made them." (Gen 6:1–7)

In this Genesis 6 myth it is the mythic "sons of God" (Nephilim, or Watchers as they are often called), who breached the boundary between heaven and earth. Evil was caused by these mythic sons of Yahweh who rebelled against Yahweh, went down to earth, had intercourse and children with earthly women, thus, corrupting humanity. In this myth, the purity of Yahweh is maintained and the blame is placed on the rebelling sons. This second myth is the prologue to the Noah flood story and the rationale for the flood. The myth pictures humanity as having become so systemically evil from the Nephilim that Yahweh wanted to destroyed it and start over again.

We see the obvious parallels between Genesis 6 and the older Gilgamesh Epic flood stories. The Hebrew flood myth, however, has a radically different understanding of God. In the biblical myth the flood comes, but Yahweh's disposition was not violence against creation, but a compassion for Noah and all the animals which could not let them be destroyed. Yahweh remembers and saves Noah, his family, and the seed of all living beings. It is this compassionate remembering that makes the Hebrews' Yahweh different from the other gods of vengeance we have been mentioning.

It is significant that although Daniel 4:17 mentions the term "Watcher," the Nephilim myth of evil is never used again in the Hebrew canon. The Hebrew canonical writers rejected this heavenly origin of evil in their understanding of humanity and kept it squarely on human choices. But the Watchers are picked up in the apocalyptic writings of 1 Enoch in the third century BCE as we shall see.

## THE ABSENCE OF EVIL IN GENESIS 1

Genesis 1, is totally different from Genesis 2–3 and 6, and was written centuries later. The setting for writing this chapter is either in captive Babylon or shortly after the exiles were freed from Babylon in 536 BCE. The exile had been a horrible experience. Their center of worship, the temple, which had for them been the place of Yahweh's home on earth, had been destroyed. Their leadership had been carried off into fifty years of exile among Babylonian pagans. The people who were left behind in destroyed Jerusalem were surviving the best they could in a chaotic world. For them systemic evil was real and they were suffering from it. Thus, coming from the Priestly tradition ("P") of Hebrew writings, chapter 1 is a carefully crafted affirmation of the Jewish understanding of their Yahweh, who in a creative act, established control over a chaotic void. In that creative act the power and goodness of Yahweh was demonstrated.

For the writer or writers of Genesis 1, this Yahweh was not many, nor divided, but One. He was the Creator of all that existed which was "good" including human beings. There is no dualism of the human being with a good soul and an evil body. The liturgical repetition at the end of each act of creation was: ". . . and God saw that it was good." This established the goodness and perfection of all creation. As the Gottingen Old Testament professor Gerhard von Rad asserts, the creation by Yahweh could be seen as completely perfect with no evil and no opposing power. All was under Yahweh's control.[2] The concepts of Genesis 2–3, with an Adam and Eve and the so-called "fall" are not mentioned.

It needs to be recognized that this Genesis 1 theological statement is not a scientific treatise concerning how creation started. If anything the seven-day sequence of the chapter may have been based on the priestly liturgical tradition of their time, i.e., six days of work, with rest for humans and their animals on the seventh. The priests patterned Yahweh's creative action based upon a liturgical pattern they had lived with for generations. The reality of a seven day week, and the sacredness of the Sabbath, were affirmed. Walter Brueggemann's insights are especially helpful:

> The original sabbath in Israel was not a day of worship but a day of rest. In the exilic period, the observance of the sabbath has special significance for exiled Israelites. It was an act which announced their faith in this God and a rejection of all other gods, religions, and world-views. . . . God does not spend the seventh day in exhaustion but in serenity and peace. In contrast to the gods of Babylon, this God is not anxious about his creation but is at ease with the well-being of his rule. It announces that the world is safely in God's hands. The world will not disintegrate if we stop our efforts. The world relies on God's promises and not our efforts. . . .

2. Rad, *Genesis*, 50.

> The sabbath is a sociological expression of *a new humanity* willed by God. Sabbath is the end of grasping and therefore the end of exploitation. Sabbath is a day of revolutionary equality in society. On that day all rest equally, regardless of wealth or power or need (Exod 20:8–11). . . . Sabbath is an unspoken prayer for the coming of a new sanity shaped by the power and graciousness of God."[3]

It is paramount to see Genesis chapter 1, not as a scientific claim, but as a theological claim for Yahweh's control over the chaotic and systemic evil the Jews were experiencing. It also established his supremacy over the future of creation until its final end. It is a theological statement about the compassion of Yahweh and the goodness of creation as a gift of the Creator to humanity. Yahweh is not vengeful. The human being is born as part of this goodness, not fallen and therefore not a sinner genetically ever after. It does not deny the existence of chaos and systemic evil against which Yahweh is in combat, but in this chapter there is no Satan, no hell, no original sin of Adam, and no curse of Adam and Eve.

It is noteworthy that in the final formation of the Hebrew Bible, this Genesis 1 creation story was placed first in the Pentateuch as the establishing statement for the Hebrews about Yahweh's power, Yahweh's compassion, and Yahweh's gift to humanity of a "perfect" creation, to use von Rad's statement above.

## CONCLUSIONS

There are three creation myths found in the Hebrew canon. In Genesis 2–3, the human is blamed for evil as a consequence of its own choice to rebel. In Genesis 6, it is the cosmic sons of God who get out of hand and cause all manner of evil. In Genesis 1, evil is not the main subject, but rather Yahweh's creative goodness and control over creation. But in the Hebrew prophets' writings, they recognized the corruption of systemic evil within their society's governance and social structure. It is this human systemic evil which will break apart the covenant made at Sinai.

However, these early Hebrews did not personalize systemic evil as a cosmic being or give it a mythic name. Nor do these three myths designate a concept of Sheol or hell. Now, it is to the Hebrew concepts of life and Sheol that we turn.

---

3. Brueggemann, *Genesis*, 35–36.

# 5

# Hebrew Myths of Life, Death, and Sheol

PEOPLE HAVE MANY QUESTIONS. Do humans simply die and that is the end of it? Is there a factor of justice and punishment at death and/or after death? I suspect for many of us we assume that the concepts of hell and Satan go together and reach back as far as history can be conceived. This is not the case. In this chapter, I will focus on life and Sheol, but will delay examining the role of Satan until the Greek occupation period when it enters as a factor.

## HEBREW CONCEPTS OF LIFE AND DEATH

Two mythical concepts are found in the Hebrew understanding of human life and death. The first is the Israelitic concept that Yahweh gave *nephish* or life to every living creature. It is used first for the lower animals in Genesis 1:20–21. The second is *ruach* which is God's breath that gives life for humans. "Then the LORD God formed man from the dust of the ground, and breathed into his nostrils the breath of life; and the man became a living being" (Gen 2:7).

Here, the pre-birth human is nothing until it is invested with Yahweh's breath. It then becomes an undivided oneness, a person. In this early tradition it is not a body with a separate soul, but a body with life from God. This body-life embryo is an indivisible unity at birth. This is in sharp contrast to a physical dualism with a good soul being incarnated into a corrupt body which we shall see later in Plato and related Greek myths. The Hebrews saw that when Yahweh's breath stops, the human body stops and individual life ends. We see this understanding in Job: "If he should take back his spirit to himself and gather to himself his breath, all flesh would perish together and all mortals return to dust" (Job 34:14–15). This would be the end of it.

## THE HEBREW SHEOL

The concept or myth of Sheol needs to be understood in light of ancient peoples' understanding of their cosmos which was conceived as a three-sphered universe. First, humans knew they lived on a solid surface which was imagined as flat and the center of the universe. Second, the ancients saw the sun, the moon and the stars moving across the sky above. They thought there must be a second sphere above which was the home of the gods. Third, the ancients also saw springs of water and molten fires of volcanos coming from below the ground. So there must be a third underworld sphere of water and fire.

Given their primitive science and knowledge it was this three-sphered universe concept that made sense to the Hebrews. Yahweh lived in the sky above, the people buried their dead in the underground sphere, in a place they called Sheol. The Hebrews thought that since they had been created out of the dust of the earth, at death the body is buried in the earth and decomposes back into dust (Gen 3:19).

The kind of existence that continued after death in Sheol was called "shades" (Ps 88:10, Isa 14: 9). This meant they were as "shadows of their former selves," without blood or breath or soul. It was a place of nothingness where the dead could not interact with the living. In early Hebrew theology all life arrived at the same destiny with no concept of individual judgment. The kings and peasants, the good and the bad, all went to Sheol as the final resting place.

This lack of individual judgment centers on the concept of community that we have already examined in chapter three. It was the community that had made a promise to Yahweh at Sinai. It was also the whole community that had strayed from the promises made. Any punishment was seen as Yahweh handing the nation over to the consequences of its own decisions which often took the path of being conquered by other nations: Assyria, Babylon, Greece, etc. This affected the whole community. Only later do we see a legal system centering on tightly defined laws that began to judge individual actions and resulted in individual judgment.

## A DEFINITION OF HELL

Alan E. Bernstein, professor of history at the University of Arizona, is helpful in defining a concept of hell. He makes a distinction between two kinds of death. The first he calls a "neutral death" where all humans die with no judgment between the just and the unjust. Sheol is this concept of death. The second, he calls a "moral death" which developed later in Greek mythology where humans are rewarded or punished in an afterlife on the basis of their life upon earth. This moral death necessitated a dying, a resurrection to life after death, a judgment, then rewards for the righteous and a final punishment for the unrighteous. It is this second concept in which there is final punishment of the wicked that Bernstein defines as "hell."[1] This fits our contemporary usage of the word, but this is not the Hebrew conception of Sheol.

Again, we need to remember that myths are stabs at trying to understand life and death. Sheol was the early Hebrew mythic concept to give meaning to death as best they could. In many ways they were not too far off target. They buried their dead and that was as far as they could witness. Mythical speculation beyond this, such as a heaven for the righteous and a separate hell for the unrighteous, was not part of their thinking. This neutral understanding of Sheol is found throughout the Hebrew canon, from Genesis to Malachi. There was no hint of a resurrection in Hebrew literature prior to the Babylonian exile of 587 BCE.

However, because of the suffering and chaos they experienced during and following the exile of 586–536 BCE, the early concepts of Sheol began to be questioned. Foreign powers had brutalized their people. Individuals, even the priests, were ignoring Yahweh, breaking the commandments, and dying unpunished. What should happen to them? In Job we find a complaint that the "wicked live on, reach old age, and grow mighty in power . . . and no rod of God is upon them. . . . They spend their days in prosperity and in peace go down to Sheol" (Job 21:7, 13). Where is Yahweh's justice if the wicked are never punished? In future chapters we will come back to the pre- and post-exile periods to look at this urgent question as raised in Habukkuk, Malachi and Jewish apocalyptic literature.

During the Persian occupation period (538 to 325 BCE) that will be examined in chapter 8, we will note the Zoroastrian concept of a Bridge of the Separator where sinners, at death, are pushed into a deep pit of punishment and the faithful are sent to a paradise. We will also note during the

---

1. Bernstein, *Formation of Hell*, 3.

Eliminating Satan and Hell

Greek occupation period (325 to 60 BCE) the influence of Plato and his concept of hell, as well as the use of Tartarus and hades in Greek myths as a finality after death. Finally, we will need to note the Jewish concepts of resurrection which appear in the Little Apocalypse of Isaiah 24–27. We will examine each of these later. However, two other important observations about Sheol must be made.

## TRANSLATING HEBREW SHEOL INTO GREEK HADES

First; when the Hebrew canon was translated into the Greek Septuagint (ca. 285 to 246 BCE), the nearest Greek term for a concept like the Hebrew Sheol was the Greek term of hades. Thus, Sheol, was translated as hades, which made a conceptual shift from the Hebrew "neutral death" with no punishment, to the Greek hades, "moral death," implying possible punishment. This meant all Jews, and the New Testament writers, who were using the Greek Septuagint as their Hebrew Scriptures were reading hades. Unfortunately, this Septuagint use of hades carried a punishing concept which is not in the basic Hebrew concept of Sheol. We wll come back to this a number of times.

Second, Sheol was used sixty-four times in the Old Testament. It was translated in the King James version thirty-one times as "hell" and twenty-nine times as "grave," two times as "pit," and once each as "darkness" or "depth." This use of "hell" gave all readers of the King James Version a concept of punishment. Again, I must emphasize, both the Septuagint and the King James Version translations give us a misunderstanding of the neutral Hebrew Sheol.

## SAVED OR LOST

Finally, for this chapter, the terms "saved" and "lost" are widely used in many contemporary religious circles as designations for after death wherein the "saved" are sent to heaven and the "lost" to hell. We need to look at how the terms were used in the Hebrew canon.

The concepts of saved, or salvation, were used almost exclusively in the Hebrew canon as being saved from disease, from death, or from a foreign enemy. Time and again in their history, Israelite cities were surrounded and put under siege by foreign troops. The Israelites were "saved" when either the foreign armies were defeated or they withdrew and the people were "saved" to go securely in an out of the city again. For the Hebrew prophets, the Messiah was to come from the household of Israel and "save" them from foreigners and reestablish a Davidic empire upon earth (see Isa 9:6 and 11:1).

Where Jewish biblical eschatology of being "saved" is found, it is centered on Yahweh's actions in reestablishing the Sinai covenant relationship on earth. There are similar allusions in Isaiah's Little Apocalypse (chapter 24:19), that when Yahweh restores Israel, the righteous dead may rise and join the renewed community. However as we shall later see, this Little Apocalypse is a very late document developed during the Greek occupation period of the Ptolemies (ca. 301 to 210 BCE). Until then, with the Hebrew biblical concepts of Sheol as a neutral place of no judgment, the concepts of being "saved" or "lost" had no theological connection to what happened to individuals at death. This is radically different from the judgmental connotations these terms carry in certain theological circles today.

## CONCLUSIONS

Bernstein makes a careful definition of hell as a place where the wicked must receive the justice of eternal punishment. No neutral location for the dead, as we have seen in previous myths, qualify because hell must punish. Early Jewish constructs of life after death stayed clear of foreign mythical concepts such as hell, saved or lost. These concepts will not emerge in any recognizable form until after the Babylonian exile. There they will be found in Jewish apocalyptic myths such as in 1 Enoch 103:5–8 where Sheol is connected to a place of darkness and flaming fire. However, these apocalyptic books were intentionally excluded from the Hebrew canon. We will study this in future chapters. Unfortunately as we have seen, in the Septuagint, Sheol was translated into the Greek as hades and used in the King James Bible as "hell," both wrongly implying a place of punishment.

In my first chapter, I indicated that one of the ultimate questions is the nature of God. Therefore, we turn away from Satan and hell in the next chapter and look to understand the Israelites' most basic experience with Yahweh, their Creator-God. Is it in the character of Yahweh to be vindictive and punitive? There is much in our contemporary literature that claims Israel's God as cruel and punishing of everyone except the Chosen Few. This was not the Hebrew picture of Yahweh that we will see.

# 6

# Yahweh
## Punitive or Compassionate?

Is Yahweh angry and punitive or compassionate, forgiving, and reconciling? The best way to tell is to do a quick survey and listen to the prophetic voices over the course of the centuries. Here we will be looking at many biblical passages that reveal the Hebrews' experience with Yahweh. For the biblical scholar these voices are not new. For the novice who has not heard them, it is my hope that they will be insightful and compelling. Our time frame is 800 to 500 BCE.

We look back at the signature event of the exodus and Sinai covenant. In the burning bush story Moses was confronted by a god named Yahweh who said: "I have observed the misery of your people. I have heard their cry. I have come to deliver them from the Egyptians" (Exod 3:7–8). For the Hebrews, their Yahweh observes, hears, and delivers. This is radically different from the gods in the *Enuma Elish* myth. The Hebrews experienced their Yahweh as a caring, compassionate, and strong enough god to take a people from the bottom of the heap and liberate them from a powerful *Enuma Elish*-type oppression of Egypt.

In the middle of the desert, the story tells us, their Yahweh makes a covenant with them, as we have seen. It is not a top-down covenant but a covenant between two equals. The holy and majestic Yahweh offers to take the Hebrew slaves into Yahweh's unending care, and they pledge their gratitude, loyalty and worship to be Yahweh's holy people. This set the tone for the Hebrews' understanding and experience as a baseline with their Yahweh down through centuries of their history, as we shall see.

## A WAYWARD PEOPLE AND VOICES OF AMOS, HOSEA, AND MICAH

It is also clear that the Hebrews broke their side of the Sinai covenant again and again, for which they are answerable to Yahweh. They were a rebellious lot. It was the northern kingdom's infidelity that drew Yahweh's sharp criticism through the voice of the prophet Amos (ca. 790–745 BCE) calling for a new faithfulness in their worship.

> I hate, I despise your festivals,
> and I take no delight in your solemn assemblies.
> Even though you offer me your burnt offerings and grain offerings,
> I will not accept them;
> and the offerings of well-being of your fatted animals
> I will not look upon.
> Take away from me the noise of your songs;
> I will not listen to the melody of your harps.
> But let justice roll down like waters,
> and righteousness like an ever-flowing stream. (Amos 5:21–24)

But a deeply disappointed Yahweh does not take away his side of the Sinai covenant.

> I will restore the fortunes of my people Israel,
> and they shall rebuild the ruined cities and inhabit them;
> they shall plant vineyards and drink their wine,
> and they shall make gardens and eat their fruit.
> I will plant them upon their land,
> and they shall never again be plucked up
> out of the land that I have given them,
> says the LORD your God. (Amos 9:14–15)

Hosea (750 to 720 BCE), another pre-exile prophet, also reminds the northern kingdom of their beginnings in Egypt: how Yahweh had led them out safely, how they had been fed in the desert, and of the covenant made at Sinai. But the people who were now fat and satisfied had forgotten their history and strayed from Yahweh. Because of this, Yahweh's voice to Israel through Hosea contained a constant tension between the deserved judgment for Israel's faithless actions on the one hand, and the forgiving, reconciling, compassionate Yahweh shown at Sinai on the other hand. We see this clearly in the following passages.

> "When Israel was a child, I loved him, and out of Egypt I called my son.
> The more I called them, the more they went from me, they kept sacrificing to the Baals, and offering incense to idols.
> Yet it was I who taught Ephriam to walk, I took them up in my arms, but they did not know that I healed them.
> I led them with cords of human kindness, with bands of love.
> I was to them like those who lifts infants to their cheeks.
> I bent down and fed them.
> They shall return to the land of Egypt, and Assyria shall be their king, because they have refused to return to me.
> The sword rages in their cities, it consumes their oracle-priests, and devours because of their schemes.
> My people are bent on turning away from me.
> To the Most High they call, but he does not raise them up at all. (Hos 11:1–7)

Was Yahweh disappointed? Yes! Was Yahweh tempted to let them go back to Egypt because they were bent on turning away from the One who loved them? Yes! But what was Yahweh's judgment, Yahweh's justice? Not the action of an Enlil who wanted to destroy the totality of humanity. Listen to Yahweh's compassion again through Hosea:

> How can I give you up, Ephriam? How can I hand you over, O Israel?
> My heart recoils within me, my compassion grows warm and tender.
> I will not execute my fierce anger;
> I will not again destroy Ephriam, for I am God, not a mere mortal, the Holy one in your midst, and I will not come in wrath."
> (Hos 11:8–9)

It should be recognized that Hosea was preaching to Israel, the northern kingdom, prior to its destruction in 732 BCE. For him Israel was full of deceit. Yet, Yahweh's sense of justice and love for Israel is the same covenantal love for her as expressed at Sinai. Yahweh does not act as mere mortals would do.

> I will love them freely,
> for my anger has turned from them.
> I will be like the dew to Israel;

> he shall blossom like the lily,
> he shall strike root like the forests of Lebanon.
> His shoots shall spread out;
> his beauty shall be like the olive tree,
> and his fragrance like that of Lebanon.
> They shall again live beneath my shadow,
> they shall flourish as a garden;
> they shall blossom like the vine,
> I will heal their disloyalty;
> their fragrance shall be like the wine of Lebanon. (Hos 14:4–7)

Here is no vindictive, punitive Yahweh. This is not a justice of anger or even of law, but a justice of deep, compassionate love for his people. Yahweh's goal was to restore a wayward Israel and bring it to life again. But the northern kingdom did not listen to Yahweh and Yahweh let them suffer the result, or wrath, of their choices, which resulted in the Assyrian capture of the kingdom and the loss of the ten northern tribes of Israel.

Meanwhile, the southern kingdom of Judah centered in Jerusalem remained intact. But again we see a wayward Judah in Yahweh's call for human responsibility through the voice of Micah (ca. 750 to 680 BCE), who shares with Hosea a sharp critique of the Hebrews, this time directed toward Jerusalem. "I have told you, O people, what is good; and what do I require of you but to do justice, and to love kindness, and to walk humbly with me, your God" (Mic 6:8).

Micah sees a Yahweh chastising his people, but not to destroy them.

> Who is a God like you, pardoning iniquity
> and passing over the transgression
> of the remnant of your possession?
> He does not retain his anger forever,
> because he delights in showing clemency.
> He will again have compassion upon us;
> he will tread our iniquities under foot.
> You will cast all our sins
> into the depths of the sea.
> You will show faithfulness to Jacob
> and unswerving loyalty to Abraham,
> as you have sworn to our ancestors
> from the days of old. (Mic 7:18–20)

In the Hebrew narrative, the prophets constantly remind the people of their pledge to the Sinai covenant. They warn, they condemn, they predict dire consequences. But they never fail to champion Yahweh's faithfulness to the covenant. Yet the people were bent on going their own way. We see this in the kingship of Manassah (ruled 687 to 642 BCE) who was seen as the worst of the kings as he built altars for Baal, delved into astrology and "has done more wicked than all that the Amorites did and has caused Judah also to sin with his idols" (2 Kgs 21:11).

In 632 BCE, King Josiah attempted to develop a new covenant with Israel and championed the return to the Lord. The book of Deuteronomy, a book of law with its restatement of the Sinai covenant (Deut 5:6–21) is the product of this reform. This particular message took pains to remind the Hebrews that it was Yahweh who had led them out of slavery; he was their singular god and "you shall have no other gods before me" (Deut 5:7). Josiah read the book of law to all the people which Hilkiah had found in the temple, and all the people re-pledged their loyalty to Yahweh (1 Kgs 23:1–3). Unfortunately, the reform was short-lived. Josiah was killed in battle in 609 BCE and Judah became a vassal state of Egypt. Then kings Jehoahaz and Jehoiakim again "did what was evil in the sight of the Lord" (2 Kgs 23:32, 36).

## JEREMIAH: A VOICE BEFORE THE 587 BCE EXILE

The southern kingdom, now called Israel, carried on until the Babylonian captivity of 587 BCE. It also had not learned its lesson. Jeremiah (ca. 627 to 587 BCE), in his poetic writings, emphasized the grief and sorrow that Yahweh endured from the unfaithful southern kingdom (Jer 4–6). Yet we see Jeremiah in chapters 31 and 32 giving voice to Yahweh's yearning to restore Israel.

> The days are surely coming, says the LORD, when I will make a new covenant with the house of Israel and the house of Judah. It will not be like the covenant that I made with their ancestors when I took them by the hand to bring them out of the land of Egypt—a covenant that they broke, though I was their husband, says the LORD. But this is the covenant that I will make with the house of Israel after those days, says the LORD: I will put my law within them, and I will write it on their hearts; and I will be their God, and they shall be my people. No longer shall they teach one another, or say to each other, "Know the LORD," for they shall all know me, from the least of them to the greatest, says the LORD;

> for I will forgive their iniquity, and remember their sin no more. (Jer 31:31–34)
>
> Now therefore thus says the LORD, the God of Israel, concerning this city of which you say, "It is being given into the hand of the king of Babylon by the sword, by famine, and by pestilence": See, I am going to gather them from all the lands to which I drove them in my anger and my wrath and in great indignation; I will bring them back to this place, and I will settle them in safety. They shall be my people, and I will be their God. I will give them one heart and one way, that they may fear me for all time, for their own good and the good of their children after them. I will make an everlasting covenant with them, never to draw back from doing good to them; and I will put the fear of me in their hearts, so that they may not turn from me. I will rejoice in doing good to them, and I will plant them in this land in faithfulness, with all my heart and all my soul. (Jer 32:36–41)

Would an angry Enlil be so intent on reestablishing an original covenant or bringing a wayward people back onto a restored relationship? No! But here is a very loving, forgiving Yahweh. Yet, Israel still strayed and Babylon captured it in 587 BCE, destroyed the temple and carried into a fifty-year exile the elite officials and Zadokite priests. Again they were a captive state and vassals to a foreign power.

## SECOND ISAIAH: CHAPTERS 40–55, YAHWEH'S DEEP COMPASSION

Listen to another voice. Second Isaiah (587 to 537 BCE), was written during the exile and held out the promise that Yahweh would bring the exiles back, the temple would be rebuilt, and the new kingdom would be established on earth. Like other passages at which we are looking, Second Isaiah voices Yahweh's singular love and compassion for Israel.

> But now thus says the LORD,
> he who created you, O Jacob,
> he who formed you, O Israel:
> Do not fear, for I have redeemed you;
> I have called you by name, you are mine.
> When you pass through the waters, I will be with you;
> and through the rivers, they shall not overwhelm you;
> when you walk through fire you shall not be burned,
> and the flame shall not consume you.

## Eliminating Satan and Hell

> For I am the LORD your God,
> the Holy One of Israel, your Savior.
> I give Egypt as your ransom,
> Ethiopia and Seba in exchange for you.
> Because you are precious in my sight,
> and honored, and I love you,
> I give people in return for you,
> nations in exchange for your life.
> Do not fear, for I am with you . . .
> I, I am He who blots out your transgressions for my own sake,
> and I will not remember your sins. (Isa 43:1–5, 25)

It is clear that Second Isaiah's confidence is that Yahweh's promise is not a punishing destruction but love. Humans may have their justice of law that demands punishment for wrong, but Yahweh has a justice of love that commands forgiveness and restoration.

It was also during the midst of the exile when Israel sharply defined it's Yahweh as different from the many gods of Babylon such as Enlil, Ishtar, Marduk, etc. Now, during the exile, the Hebrew priests boldly declared Yahweh was the one and only God.

> I am the LORD, and there is no other;
> besides me there is no god.
> I arm you, though you do not know me,
> so that they may know, from the rising of the sun
> and from the west, that there is no one besides me;
> I am the LORD, and there is no other.
> I form light and create darkness,
> I make weal and create woe;
> I the LORD do all these things. (Isa 45:5–7)

This proclamation declared Yahweh as not only the Creator-God of the universe, but the origin of all historical events. This, however, made a heavy load for Hebrew theology to carry. If Yahweh is all good, how do they explain evil? We shall see in Persian Zoroastrianism, Ahura Mazda is also proclaimed the one and only monotheistic god. However, since Ahura Mazda could not do evil, two lesser gods are proclaimed. Spenta Mainyu, a good god, and Angra Mainyu, an evil god. The Hebrews never went this direction.

We also remember that Genesis chapter 1 was written during this same period of the Babylonian exile. In the midst of the exile's chaos and pain, even in the midst of the systemic evil they were experiencing, it was still the

Jews' conviction that Yahweh was compassionate, what he had created was perfect, and he was still in complete control to eventually eliminate all evil. Furthermore, Yahweh's caring, sustaining compassion was not for the Israelites alone, but for all nations. Here, in the midst of a depressing exile, is reaffirmed the covenantal concept of Yahweh's graciousness as established in the co-commitments at Sinai.

## MALACHI RAISES QUESTIONS

The leaders returned from exile in 537 BCE, the temple was rebuilt, yet all was not well. Israel had gone back to its old ways. Malachi (ca. 500 to 450 BCE) raises serious questions on behalf of God.

> A son honors his father, and servants their master. If then I am a father, where is the honor due me? And if I am a master, where is the respect due me? says the LORD of hosts to you, O priests, who despise my name. You say, "How have we despised your name?" By offering polluted food on my altar. And you say, "How have we polluted it?" By thinking that the LORD's table may be despised. When you offer blind animals in sacrifice, is that not wrong? And when you offer those that are lame or sick, is that not wrong? Try presenting that to your governor; will he be pleased with you or show you favor? says the LORD of hosts. And now implore the favor of God, that he may be gracious to us. The fault is yours. Will he show favor to any of you? says the LORD of hosts. Oh, that someone among you would shut the temple doors, so that you would not kindle fire on my altar in vain! I have no pleasure in you, says the LORD of hosts, and I will not accept an offering from your hands. (Mal 1:6–10)

Systemic evil has taken over again and infected the priesthood and the patterns of the temple. The whole system had become so evil that Malachi felt it needed to be shut down!

## THIRD ISAIAH: CHAPTER 56–66

Yet, in Third Isaiah (ca. 538 to 450 BCE) we hear again Yahweh's compassionate yearning and hunger to fully restore Israel to their covenantal promise.

> I was ready to be sought out by those who did not ask,
>   to be found by those who did not seek me.

### Eliminating Satan and Hell

> I said, "Here I am, here I am," to a nation that did not call on my name.
> I held out my hands all day long to a rebellious people who walk in a way that is not good, following their own devices; a people who continually provoke me to my face. (Isa 65:1–3)

Could there ever be a more loving plea to a wayward people? Or, can there ever be a more tender promise than the following?

> For I am about to create new heavens
> and a new earth;
> the former things shall not be remembered
> or come to mind.
> But be glad and rejoice for ever
> in what I am creating;
> for I am about to create Jerusalem as a joy,
> and its people as a delight.
> I will rejoice in Jerusalem,
> and delight in my people;
> no more shall the sound of weeping be heard in it,
> or the cry of distress.
> No more shall there be in it
> an infant that lives but a few days,
> or an old person who does not live out a lifetime;
> for one who dies at a hundred years will be considered a youth,
> and one who falls short of a hundred will be considered accursed.
> They shall build houses and inhabit them;
> they shall plant vineyards and eat their fruit.
> They shall not build and another inhabit;
> they shall not plant and another eat;
> for like the days of a tree shall the days of my people be,
> and my chosen shall long enjoy the work of their hands.
> They shall not labour in vain,
> or bear children for calamity;
> for they shall be offspring blessed by the Lord—
> and their descendants as well.
> Before they call I will answer,
> while they are yet speaking I will hear.
> The wolf and the lamb shall feed together,
> the lion shall eat straw like the ox;
> but the serpent—its food shall be dust!
> They shall not hurt or destroy
> on all my holy mountain,
> says the Lord. (Isa 65:17–25)

## CONCLUSIONS

This is an important chapter in seeing the Hebrew prophets' consistent understanding of their god. The goal of Yahweh was to bring about a new Jerusalem, an earthly community of Israel that would be peaceful, just and holy . . . a renewed Sinai covenant. We see no concepts of a Satan as an enemy of Yahweh in these passages. We see no battle where Yahweh will use violence to destroy all on earth and start over again. In these passages we see that it is in the character of Yahweh to love, to be forgiving, to reconcile. Yahweh is not a punitive god who would destroy Israel in an eternal hell. This is in sharp contrast to cultural systems we have seen where people serve the gods as in the *Emuna Elish* myth and are slaves of the powerful. This is also a radically different understanding of Yahweh from what we see expressed in the punishing creeds of many contemporary religious communities where Satan is God's enemy and God, in anger, will exile to eternal punishment all who do not believe a certain theological way.

This chapter also reveals a more accurate understanding of Israel's "Yahweh" than many of the current more negative portrayals of the so-called "New Atheists," such as Victor Stenger's *The New Atheism*, Richard Dawkin's *The God Delusion*, or Christopher Hitchins, *God Is Not Great*. However, it is to the credit of these critical writers that they are raising fundamental questions, which challenges a frozen biblical literalism and forces new paradigms of biblical understanding.

The baseline in understanding the Creator-God, and the Hebrews' responsibility, is the Sinai covenant of mutual commitments, both between Yahweh and the people, and between the people to each other. It is important for us to keep this Hebrew covenantal concept before us when we look at Paul's and Jesus' concept of the kingdom of God.

Yet, the exile raised profound questions for the Hebrews about the nation's future. Ezekiel will raise the image of a new Davidic empire with Yahweh as King in Jerusalem. Third Isaiah will raise the image of a Servant Israel, a teaching light to the nations. It is to these insights we turn next.

# 7

# Israel, a Monarchy or Servant?

IN THE LAST CHAPTER we saw the Hebrew prophets' confidence that Yahweh would stand with them and bring Israel to a new future. But what is Israel's future? King David was the national hero and the symbol of an ideal nation. Would a new Davidic empire arise? Even during the period before the exile with its series of bad kings and their systemic evil, Habukkuk (610–587 BCE) raised serious questions regarding when Yahweh would act to save Iarael (Hab 1:2). But Yahweh did not save them from the exile, as we have seen, but allowed the nation to suffer the consequences of its own choices and unfaithfulness.

## THE BABYLONIAN EXILE: 587 TO 537 BCE

The ensuing exile that began in 587 BBE was a tragic blow and a hard lesson for Israel to understand. The Babylonian King Nebuchadnezzer laid utter waste to every important town of Judah, destroying Jerusalem and the temple in August 587 BCE (2 Kgs 25; Jer 39). Many towns were never reinhabited. The religious and political leadership had been carried to Babylon. The survivors in Judah were left prey to pillaging from hostile neighbors. The brutal reality was that the messiah had not come and the Hebrews were still getting beaten up. Systemic evil became rampant in the political hierarchy and the Second Temple became idolatrous. Where was their Yahweh who had promised in the Sinai covenant that those who remained faithful would not be forgotten?

*Israel, a Monarchy or Servant?*

This long period of occupation history from 587 to 60 BCE is largely unfamiliar to most of us. Many of us jump from Jeremiah and Isaiah to the birth of Jesus in 6 BCE and leave this turbulent period of Jewish history largely untouched and unknown. Israel had to come to terms with the fact that their political leadership, which included the Zadokite priesthood, was carried into Babylon for fifty years. By 537 BCE it became apparent that the Persian ruler, Cyrus, would capture Babylon and allow the exiles to return to Jerusalem.

In this chapter, I want us to examine the changing role projected for Israel in the books of Ezekiel and Isaiah as they came to grips with this tragic period and its aftermath. We will be looking further at the nature of Yahweh and the role of Israel, but only indirectly at the role of Sheol and Satan.

## EZEKIEL: 595 TO 563 BCE

The prophet Ezekiel, as part of the exiled group, had to face the reality of a destroyed Jerusalem and a destroyed temple. How could he and Israel come to terms with Yahweh's failure to protect Yahweh's own holy place? Speaking to Israel during the midst of the exile, Ezekiel expressed Yahweh's clear disappointment. In chapter 10:15–19 Ezekiel portrays Yahweh abandoning the temple because it had become impure and profane. Israel deserved to be destroyed. They had brought such pollution and unholiness to Israel that Ezekiel felt the holy Yahweh could no longer inhabit Jerusalem and the temple.

> The word of the LORD came to me: Mortal, say to it: You are a land that is not cleansed, not rained upon in the day of indignation. Its princes within it are like a roaring lion tearing the prey; they have devoured human lives; they have taken treasure and precious things; they have made many widows within it. Its priests have done violence to my teaching and have profaned my holy things; they have made no distinction between the holy and the common, neither have they taught the difference between the unclean and the clean, and they have disregarded my sabbaths, so that I am profaned among them. Its officials within it are like wolves tearing the prey, shedding blood, destroying lives to get dishonest gain. Its prophets have smeared whitewash on their behalf, seeing false visions and divining lies for them, saying, "Thus says the Lord GOD," when the LORD has not spoken. The people of the

land have practiced extortion and committed robbery; they have oppressed the poor and needy, and have extorted from the alien without redress. And I sought for anyone among them who would repair the wall and stand in the breach before me on behalf of the land, so that I would not destroy it; but I found no one. Therefore I have poured out my indignation upon them; I have consumed them with the fire of my wrath; I have returned their conduct upon their heads, says the Lord God. (Ezek 22:23–31)

Ezekiel was convinced that Yahweh had left Israel and handed her over to the destruction of its own choices. Since Yahweh's reputation had also been profaned in the sight of other nations, Yahweh must act decisively to also show the pagan nations that Yahweh would not tolerate such infidelity. By destroying Jerusalem it also restored Yahweh's reputation to other nations that the holy God can and will act against the profane. Ezekiel also saw Yahweh's opportunity to begin a new chapter in Israel's life.

In chapter 34 we see Yahweh abandoning the kings, the priests, the officials who had been the rulers of Israel. Now Yahweh would become its shepherd. "I myself will be the shepherd of my sheep, and I will make them lie down, says the Lord GOD. I will seek the lost, and I will bring back the strayed, and I will bind up the injured, and I will strengthen the weak, but the fat and the strong I will destroy. I will feed them with justice" (Ezek 34:15–16).

Henceforth, Yahweh will be the Shepherd-King who rules with compassion and justice for the whole nation, not just for the elite. Under Yahweh, human rulers will only be princes, not kings. In the final chapters 40–48, Ezekiel sees Yahweh establishing a new home for Yahweh centered in a new temple that will be built following the return of the exiles from Babylon. The details of the temple are explicit and they wall out anything that is not holy. In chapter 43, the holy Yahweh is projected as inhabiting the new temple forever. "Mortal, this is the place of my throne and the place for the soles of my feet, where I will reside among the people of Israel forever. The house of Israel shall no more defile my holy name, neither they nor their kings, by their whoring, and by the corpses of their kings at their death. . . . Now let them put away their idolatry and the corpses of their kings far from me, and I will reside among them forever" (Ezek 43:7, 9).

Jerusalem will be Yahweh's Holy City, the temple will be Yahweh's holy home. Ezekiel, a Zadok priest, also projects the reestablishment of the Zadok priesthood to be the temple ministers of Yahweh. This will effectively give the Zadok priesthood an aura of holiness and unquestioned legitimacy

*Israel, a Monarchy or Servant?*

with the power to decide what is of Yahweh and what is not, what is righteous and what is evil. The "Holiness Code" of Leviticus was being developed during this period that then became the measure of faithfulness based on the strict laws and statutes of the Torah as defined by the Zadok priests. When the Zadok priests had returned they claimed this priestly prerogative as a divine right. We will see in the next chapter the ugly conflict this eventually brought about between the Zadok priests and the Levite priests, and between the Zadoks and the people.

However, several points need to be made. First, in his two apocalyptic chapters, 38 and 39, Ezekiel uses the name "Gog" as the symbol of other nations that will rise against Israel in the future. But since Yahweh's home is centered in Jerusalem never again will it be destroyed. All the hordes of Gog will be buried in the Valley of Hamon-gog (Ezek 39:12). This is not a Tartarus or hades, but simply a valley outside of Jerusalem later called gehenna. We will want to remember this gehenna term, for it is used extensively in the Christian gospels.

Second, Ezekiel began to see humanity as so contaminated by systemic evil that a holy restoration could not be accomplished by humans alone. Yahweh would have to intervene at some point after the exiles' return to destroy the evil that Ezekiel symbolizes in his use of the mythic name of "Gog" for evil. Chapters 38–39 picture a battle between God and Gog which ends the present order and the beginning of a new era of peace. We need to flag this mythical battle with Yahweh as a warrior god because its apocalyptic concept is also seen in Joel, in the Qumran writings, and the New Testament book of Revelation.

The final point we need to flag is in chapters 31–32 when Ezekiel uses a tree as a symbol for Egypt that will be cut down and thrown into the Pit of Sheol. This is consistent with the definition of Sheol we have seen before as an underground burial place, now also for apostate nations such as Egypt. But here Sheol is also connected to "the Pit." Is the Pit the same as the Valley of Gehenna which was the burial pit outside Jerusalem? Ezekiel seems to be saying so by connecting Sheol, the Pit, and gehenna as the place where the wicked will be punished.

The writer of Second Isaiah (587–537 BCE) sees something quite different from Ezekiel's Yahweh destroying the nation and starting anew. Second Isaiah understood the Jewish nation was not to be destroyed, but to remain intact and had the task of bringing justice to the Gentiles in a way

Eliminating Satan and Hell

that would show the Gentiles that their gods amounted to nothing. Yahweh alone is God and there is no other. But how?

## THE SERVANT SONGS: ISAIAH 42 AND 52-53

There are two passages in Second Isaiah that commend special attention. They show a new calling for Israel as a servant. They are also used by Jesus, and New Testament writers turned to them in their understanding of him. First is the Servant Song in Second Isaiah 42:1–4, which is an important clue to Isaiah's understanding of a gentle, healing God. Part of this passage was used at Jesus' baptism as the Spirit proclaimed him Yahweh's Son. Israel is to show the Gentiles that Yahweh is the sovereign God by being a servant nation which will bring justice to all.

> Here is my servant [nation], whom I uphold,
> my chosen, in whom my soul delights;
> I have put my spirit upon him;
> he will bring forth justice to the nations.
> He will not cry or lift up his voice,
> or make it heard in the street;
> a bruised reed he will not break,
> and a dimly burning wick he will not quench;
> he will faithfully bring forth justice.
> He will not grow faint or be crushed
> until he has established justice in the earth;
> and the coastlands wait for his teaching. (Isa 42:1–4)

Here I follow the view of the *New Revised Standard Version Study Bible* (NRSV) in its footnote that the "servant" is the nation of Israel, not a specific individual.[1] Second Isaiah's first three words of the Song designates Israel as the servant whom Yahweh had chosen. In this passage Yahweh's spirit is upon this Servant-nation for defined tasks, each of which centers on justice. In chapter 42:1, it is "to bring forth justice to the nations." In chapter 42:3, it is to "bring forth justice faithfully," and in chapter 42:4, it is "until it establishes justice in the earth and the coastlands wait for his teaching."

The New Israel's role is not to be a dominating military power, but as a quiet-spoken, gentle servant, a teacher, who will not bruise a broken reed (Isa 42:3). This is the essence of humility, but not of weak humility. It

---

1. NRSV, footnote to Isa 42:1.

## Israel, a Monarchy or Servant?

is a humility that will not "grow faint" nor allow itself to be "crushed" until justice is established not only in Palestine but "in the earth" (Isa 42:4). The task is expansive beyond Israel to all nations. The writer of Second Isaiah is convinced the nations "wait for this teaching." But how? Here we look again at Isaiah:

> I am the LORD, I have called you in righteousness,
> I have taken you by the hand and kept you;
> I have given you as a covenant to the people,
> a light to the nations,
> to open the eyes that are blind,
> to bring out the prisoners from the dungeon,
> from the prison those who sit in darkness. (Isa 42:6–7)

In their manner of living, their worship of Yahweh, Israel is to be a teaching light that opens the eyes of nations groping in the darkness. One cannot stress enough Isaiah's word "teaching" in verse 42:4. "The coastlands wait for his teaching." Israel is proclaimed, not as a powerful ruler, but as a Teacher! University of Heidelberg professor Claus Westermann comments that the nations are already anxiously looking for the kind of justice that the Servant Israel is called to bring.[2]

Here we see an expansion of Yahweh's love to all nations. This is a radical change from prior pictures of Israel's hatred toward neighbors as enemies to be destroyed. Second Isaiah's understanding is that Yahweh not only still loves Israel, but is a tender, healing, reconciling God who has compassion even for Gentile nations. Furthermore, Israel is to be a teaching servant to all nations by its humble acts of devotion and service. This is the opposite of the murderous Marduk in the *Enuma Elish* myth. It is a reversal of how Israel had seen itself in the past, and also a reversal of the punishing attitude Israel had for Gentile nations.

The second special passage is the Fourth Servant Song in Second Isaiah 52:13—53:15, often called the "Suffering Servant" passage. It begins with a promise to Servant Israel. It will not be destroyed by a punishing God but rather it will be lifted up and exalted. The connection between Isaiah chapters 42 and 53 is evident. We saw chapter 42:1 begins, "Here is my servant." We see 52:13 begin, "See, my servant."

> See, my servant shall prosper;
> he shall be exalted and lifted up,
> and shall be very high.

2. Westermann, *Isaiah 40–66*, 96.

## Eliminating Satan and Hell

> Just as there were many who were astonished at him
> —so marred was his appearance, beyond human semblance,
> and his form beyond that of mortals—
> so he shall startle many nations;
> kings shall shut their mouths because of him;
> for that which had not been told them they shall see,
> and that which they had not heard they shall contemplate. (Isa 52:13–15)

Again, the NRSV sees the Servant as being the nation of Israel, not an individual.[3] Growing out of the dry ground of captivity in Egypt, Israel was nothing to be admired. It was despised, rejected, suffered, held of no account. It was seen as stricken by Yahweh and lost like sheep who had chosen their own way. Yet through Israel's humiliation and suffering, even through Yahweh's letting them be crushed in the exile, Yahweh's ultimate will is to lift them up and exalt them above all kings (Isa 52:13–15). Here again is another reversal. The rejected, beaten down, exiled nation would rise again to be the exalted teacher of all nations.

## ISAIAH 55: YAHWEH'S PARDON

Second Isaiah ends in chapter 55 with the writer's ultimate conviction about Yahweh's call for Israel to return to Yahweh and find Yahweh's love and pardon for them.

> Seek the LORD while he may be found,
> call upon him while he is near;
> let the wicked forsake their way,
> and the unrighteous their thoughts;
> let them return to the LORD, that he may have mercy on them,
> and to our God, for he will abundantly pardon.
> For my thoughts are not your thoughts,
> nor are your ways my ways, says the LORD.
> For as the heavens are higher than the earth,
> so are my ways higher than your ways
> and my thoughts than your thoughts.( Isa 55:6-9)

In these two Servant Songs of Second Isaiah, it is clear that Israel's hope is for a rule of Yahweh on earth. This is a rule of Yahweh, not of a politically dominating nation role for Israel. These passages do not imply

---

3. NRSV, footnote to Isa 52:13.

some far-off, otherworldly, cataclysmic battle with evil at the end of history, but a restoration of Israel as a servant within the earthly time frame of Israel. Isaiah's voice is a final comforting, reassuring proclamation that Yahweh will gather the exiles back to Jerusalem. We see this in two significant passages:

> Comfort, O comfort my people, says your God. Speak tenderly to Jerusalem, and cry to her that she has served her term, that her penalty is paid, that she has received from the LORD's hand double for all her sins. (Isa 40:1–2)
>
> Do not fear, for you will not be ashamed; do not be discouraged, for you will not suffer disgrace; for you will forget the shame of your youth, and the disgrace of your widowhood you will remember no more. For your Maker is your husband, the LORD of hosts is his name; the Holy One of Israel is your Redeemer, the God of the whole earth he is called. For the LORD has called you like a wife forsaken and grieved in spirit, like the wife of a man's youth when she is cast off, says your God. For a brief moment I abandoned you, but with great compassion I will gather you. In overflowing wrath for a moment I hid my face from you, but with everlasting love I will have compassion on you, says the LORD, your Redeemer. (Isa 54:4–8)

## CONCLUSIONS

It is crucial to see, even coming out of the sufferings and systemic evil of the exile, that the Hebrews retained their understanding of a compassionate, forgiving Yahweh in these passages. We have seen two visions: Ezekiel's vision of a holy Yahweh, intolerant of the systemic corruption and idolatry of Israel, who lets them be destroyed in order for Yahweh to create a new nation centered in a cleansed temple, Yahweh's new home. Yahweh was to be Israel's Shepherd-King; the priests were to be subservient.

In contrast, Isaiah's vision is not a new, powerful Davidic kingdom. Rather he looks ahead for Israel to be a humble teaching servant for all nations . . . a teaching the nations eagerly await. The vision of punishment is Yahweh allowing Israel to suffer the consequences of her own past choices because she had wandered far from the relationship established in the Sinai covenant. It is a corporate punishment of the nation, not of individuals. We see in these significant passages an understanding of Yahweh far different from an angry god sending individual sinners to an eternal punishment.

## Eliminating Satan and Hell

The Satan and hell myths are not here. We turn next to the Persian period of occupation that began in 537 BCE.

# 8

# Persian Myths and the Introduction of Satan

## CYRUS

In 537 BCE, Cyrus, the Persian emperor, freed the Jewish captives from Babylon and allowed them return to Palestine. For the next two hundred years the Jews were basically under Persian rule until 325 BCE when Alexander the Great conquered the area. We know from biblical sources that Cyrus was seen as a benevolent king in allowing the Jewish exiles to return. He also encouraged them to rebuild their temple and continue in their religious beliefs and practices. He was even hailed by biblical writers as God's "anointed," a messianic person, one who saved them from the enemies of Israel (Isa 45:1–2). I will begin by examining the Persian myths of life and death that they carried with them into Israel.

## ZOROASTRIAN MYTHS

During this Persian period we have no clear picture of what influence, if any, the religion of Zoroaster had upon the Jews. One doubts, however, if the proximity of the friendly Persian rulers for over two hundred years (536 to 325 BCE) could have passed the people of Israel without leaving traces of Persian literature, language, law, and all other aspects of their civilization. Scholars differ widely on when Zoroaster lived. Until the late seventeenth century, Zoroaster was generally dated to about the sixth century BCE. However an earlier date is now considered by Iranian scholars since the social customs described in the Gathas roughly coincide with what is known of other prehistorical peoples between the thirteenth to eleventh centuries BCE. Thus, the contemporary Zoroasterian scholar Mary Boyce finds Zoroaster living sometime between 1400 to 1200 BCE in what is now modern Iran.[1]

Iranian priests held that originally there was only one plant, one animal, and one man, and from this there could only be one eternal and uncreated God who was the source of everything. Zoroaster called this beneficent Being, who created the world, Ahura Mazda. There were six other lesser deities called Spentas. Among these Spentas were two spirits, Spenta Mainyu and Angra Mainyu. These two original spirits made choices. Spenta Mainyu made a choice for good. Angra Mainyu embodied the choice of a spirit of evil who turns against every good thing Spenta Mainyu does. Thus, the earth is the battleground between these two forces.

Zoroastrianism has a full cycle of human life. Souls are placed within human bodies. Humans are then responsible for their choice either to live righteous lives following Spenta Mainyu or unrighteous lives following Angra Mainyu. The Zoroastrian concept of death was based upon which choice was made with a reward of paradise for the good; punishment for the wicked in an eternal hell. There is a point of judgment at death. As Boyce tells it, all people—men, women, servants—may obtain paradise, but they must first cross the "Bridge of the Separator." While on the bridge their ethical achievements are weighed on a scale, the soul's thoughts, words, and deeds. If the good acts are heavier, the soul is judged worthy of paradise. If the scales sink on the bad side, the bridge contracts to the width of a blade's edge, and a horrid hag seizes the soul in its arms and plunges it down to hell where the wicked endure a long age of misery, darkness, bad food, and woe. The concept of hell is presided over by Angra Mainyu.[2]

Within Zoroastrianism there is a Savior called Soshyant, or Soashyant, who will come to make the world wonderful again and then the dead shall rise up. At the end of time there is a final judgment, a final destruction of Angra Mainyu, and the last vestige of evil is eliminated. The myth answers

1. Boyce, *Zoroastrians*, 2.
2. Ibid., 27.

## Persian Myths and the Introduction of Satan

the theodicy question of why there is evil by blaming Angra Mainyu and without blaming Ahura Mazda. It also answers the human desire for justice that the wicked receive punishment, if not in this life then after death. This is done with a resurrection to paradise as a reward for the righteous and the torment of hell for the unjust. Here the self-defined righteous get the satisfaction of revenge. It is also here that we begin to see a parallel with a Satan figure in Angra Mainyu that is later developed as hostile to both God and humanity.

The Zoroastrian myth raises many questions. Why did the Persian myth makers develop this type of myth? We will never know for sure, but we may venture several speculations. One, it was a restless and turbulent time of warring chieftains. The conflict they were experiencing may have been so persistent that they could never project Ahura Mazda as being in complete control, thus there must be a separate force of evil which they named as Angra Mainyu. Two, a natural human trait would want revenge whenever a neighboring chief pillaged one's village, wantonly killing men, women and children. If justice was not accomplished in this life, why not project an after-life hell where the gods would inflict revengeful pain on one's enemy? Thus, the Bridge of the Separator makes a good myth, with the righteous being rewarded with paradise and the evil pushed into hell.

It is clear that there is in Zoroastrian mythology a Satan figure in Angra Mainyu and also what may be their first concept of hell. The focus is upon individual wrongdoing and individual punishment, not on the sin of the whole community as in the Hebrew story. Various sources indicate there were Persian influences upon the Greeks as found in Plato's *Alcibiades I* where Zoroaster is mentioned. More on this later in chapter 10. The Persian myths were in the Jewish neighborhood for two hundred years and may have helped answer Malachi's question on why the wicked were not being punished. Yet, it appears that the Jewish search for their responses looked back to their own historical Scriptures. So it is to their Jewish literature of this period that we now turn.

## BIBLICAL BOOKS WRITTEN

Following the fifty years of exile in Babylon by the Jewish leadership, their return to Jerusalem was an active time of new writings as can be seen by the following:
- Ezra-Nehemiah after 538 BCE

- Third Isaiah (chs. 56–66) ca. 520 to 510 BCE
- Haggai ca. 520 BCE
- Job ca. 500 to 400 BCE
- Zechariah 1–8 ca. 520 to 518 BCE
- Zechariah 9–14 possibly after 325 BCE
- Malachi ca. 500 to 450 BCE
- Chronicles ca. 500 to 450 BCE
- Joel ca. 400 to 350 BCE
- Jonah 4th to 5th century BCE
- Daniel was not written until ca. 165 BCE

But it was also a period in Hebrew history when, again, things did not go as expected and their confident understanding of Yahweh was shaken. They raised disturbing cries for help that we see in this communal lament of Third Isaiah.

> Look down from heaven and see,
> from your holy and glorious habitation.
> Where are your zeal and your might?
> The yearning of your heart and your compassion?
> They are withheld from me.
> For you are our father,
> though Abraham does not know us
> and Israel does not acknowledge us;
> you, O Lord, are our father;
> our Redeemer from of old is your name.
> Why, O Lord, do you make us stray from your ways
> and harden our heart, so that we do not fear you?
> Turn back for the sake of your servants,
> for the sake of the tribes that are your heritage.
> Your holy people took possession for a little while;
> but now our adversaries have trampled down your sanctuary.
> We have long been like those whom you do not rule,
> like those not called by your name.
> O that you would tear open the heavens and come down,
> so that the mountains would quake at your presence. (Isa 63:15—64:1)

*Persian Myths and the Introduction of Satan*

## THE REALITY IN JERUSALEM

To understand this lament, we need to know what was happening in their history. Prior to the exile, the Zadokite temple priests who were carried off to Babylon were the primary power group in liturgical and political affairs in Israel. When they returned fifty years later they claimed the right to resume this role. This was acceptable to the Persians as long as the Hebrews did not challenge Persian authority. Thus, the Persians and Zadokites priests collaborated together and there was a political peace during the occupation.

While the Zadokite priests were in Babylon they faced a situation of no homeland and no temple around which their faith could be maintained. They had turned, therefore, to their basic Scriptures, the Torah, to keep themselves as a "holy seed" the remnant of Yahweh's faithful people. When they returned to Jerusalem, the Torah (the Law of Moses in the Pentateuch) became the measure of fidelity. Upon their arrival in Jeruslam the Zadokite priests claimed that Yahweh had tabernacled with them in Babylon, not with those who were left behind in Jerusalem. Therefore they claimed to be *the* legitimate priests. This was not acceptable to the "left-behind" Levites, nor to the people who had remained in Jerusalem and had tried to remain faithful to Yahweh in every respect. This was a serious blow to the Levite priests.

Furthermore, in an attempt to purify their people the Zadokite priests moved to outlaw all marriages with foreign wives who were seen to corrupt the faith, and thus, such marriage must be ended. This was another severe blow to many faithful Jewish families. Also the Zadokites tried to control the ownership of the land and taxes upon the peasants on the land. These measures, and many others, marginalized and disenfranchised both the power, the income, and sense of faithfulness of the Levites and the people who had tilled the land during the exile. Now, the left-behind population began to see the Zadokite priesthood as domineering, elitist, and corrupt.

The Zadokite priests, nevertheless, rebuilt the temple with Persian encouragement and Persian money. This gave additional offense to those who had remained in Jerusalem, for they now saw the new temple being built to the glory of the Persian king, not to Yahweh. This action stirred more resentment from the left-behind peasants who viewed the Zadokite leadership as being totally corrupted by Persian pagans. Now the temple had been rebuilt, but Yahweh's promised messiah still had not come. This absence led to a firm conviction by the peasants and the visionary prophetic group to conclude that the reason the messiah had not come was because Yahweh was angry with the Zadokite priestly-political hierarchy.

The people had to face the hard fact that they were still getting beaten up, there continued to be corruption in the hierarchy, and the worship in the temple had again become idolatrous. It is in Zechariah that we now see Yahweh pleading with the people to return to Yahweh and not be like their evil ancestors before the exile (Zech 1:1–6). But prophets such as Zechariah and Third Isaiah saw no hope of this happening without a direct intervention of Yahweh.

## NEW HEAVEN AND A NEW EARTH

It is not known when Third Isaiah (chs. 55–66) was written but it is clear that it was years after chapters 40–55 and after the exiles' return. The writer of Third Isaiah foresaw the only solution to the existing corruption would be for Yahweh to create a whole new "heaven and a new earth." The writer has Yahweh proclaiming:

> For I am about to create new heavens and a new earth; the former things shall not be remembered or come to mind. But be glad and rejoice forever in what I am creating; for I am about to create Jerusalem as a joy, and its people as a delight. I will rejoice in Jerusalem, and delight in my people; no more shall the sound of weeping be heard in it, or the cry of distress. No more shall there be in it an infant that lives but a few days, or an old person who does not live out a lifetime; for one who dies at a hundred years will be considered a youth, and one who falls short of a hundred will be considered accursed. They shall build houses and inhabit them; they shall plant vineyards and eat their fruit.
> . . . Before they call I will answer, while they are yet speaking I will hear. The wolf and the lamb shall feed together, the lion shall eat straw like the ox; but the serpent—its food shall be dust. They shall not hurt or destroy on all my holy mountain, says the Lord. (Isa 65:17–25)

This does not imply a revengeful destruction of the old creation, but that God will renew the existing heaven and earth. As such, this is another expansive vision of Yahweh's activity and a new hope for all people. This renewing event was to happen on earth within Israel's time frame. But it will need Yahweh's intervention for it to occur. Third Isaiah closes chapter 66 with the positive image of Yahweh's renewed Israel, a renewed Jerusalem,

*Persian Myths and the Introduction of Satan*

and all the nations coming to Zion (Isa 66:18–24). Many scholars feel chapter 66 is a late addition to Third Isaiah. Nevertheless, all nations, expressed as "all flesh," are to worship before Yahweh every new moon and Sabbath.

But on whose terms? Who are the righteous and who are the unjust? Will all nations need to conform to the strict interpretation of being righteous as measured by the Torah law? As we have seen, the powerful Zadokite elite saw the unjust as those who opposed them and who ignored the law. This included the peasant people-of-the-land (the *am ha aretz*) and all foreign nations. Contrariwise, those who had been left behind in Jerusalem saw the powerful Zadokite elite as the thoroughly unjust. The righteous-unrighteous division was now within the Hebrew community. However, there is still no Satan, no eternal punishment in Sheol coming in a day of judgment.

## MALACHI: NO PUNISHMENT OF THE WICKED?

We saw earlier that before the exile the writer of Habakkuk (ca. 608 to 598 BCE) had also raised questions of why Yahweh seemed so silent when the wicked were swallowing up the righteous. Malachi (ca. 500 to 450 BCE), writing after the return from exile, was also echoing the same crucial questions. The nobles and religious leaders were again quick to stray from holiness and go after pleasure and gain. Furthermore, the priests were corrupting worship in the temple (Mal 1–2). Others, according to Malachi, began saying it was vain to serve Yahweh since there was no profit in keeping Yahweh's commandments when the disobedient seemed better off than the obedient. Evildoers not only prospered, but when they put Yahweh to the test, the sinners died happy with no just punishment of the wicked in this life (Mal 3:13–15). As long as there was no judgment in Sheol there was no satisfactory answer for the people. Malachi may have known the Zoroastrian solution to justice, but all he could answer was to be patient, the day is coming when all the arrogant and all evildoers will be destroyed in this life (Mal 4:1–5).

The Deuteronomic theology had implied that once the temple was rebuilt a new Davidic king would emerge from the people and a freed, restored Israel would come about. This was not happening. The confidence of the people began to fade. The widespread corruption of both the political elite and temple leadership was such that the people could not reform it or disempower it. God must come and overthrow this evil, but that will require a cosmic judgment that will terminate the old moral order and its evil, and then the creation of a new heaven and a new earth.

## JOEL: A DAY OF JUDGMENT

Joel (ca. 400 to 350 BCE) was written toward the end of the Persian period. At the time there had been a devastating invasion of locusts in the country. The book is significant in our study for the language that Joel adds to the day of judgment. On "that day" there will be earthquakes, the sun and moon will be darkened, the stars will stop shining. The Lord will head a powerful army like never seen before (Joel 2:11). This army and a powerful fire will destroy the enemy foreign nations. Tyre and Sidon will be destroyed, Egypt and Edom will become a desolate wilderness because of what they have done to Judah (3:19). A repentant Israel, however, will be spared.

> You shall eat in plenty and be satisfied,
> and praise the name of the LORD your God,
> who has dealt wondrously with you.
> And my people shall never again be put to shame.
> You shall know that I am in the midst of Israel,
> and that I, the LORD, am your God and there is no other.
> And my people shall never again be put to shame. (Joel 2:26–27)

The writers in the later Qumran community, and some New Testament writers, will pick up the apocalyptic language of Joel's army of God battling hostile forces, of earthquakes, the darkening of the sun, moon and stars. But in Joel, the day of judgment and the restoration of Judah will happen on this earth during their time frame, not at the end of history.

## INTRODUCING THE HEBREW HASSATAN (SATAN)

It was during this exile that Second Isaiah had declared a monotheistic Yahweh who was in control of everything. Whatever happened, good and bad, was attributed to Yahweh.

> I am the LORD, and there is no other.
> I form light and create darkness,
> I make weal [goodness] and create woe [evil];
> I the LORD do all these things. (Isa 45:6b–7)

## Persian Myths and the Introduction of Satan

The promises made during the exile of a glorious return and a whole new beginning of shalom and prosperity had not come. Adversity, corruption, and idolatry still reigned. This disappointing reality needed to be addressed in a way that protected the oneness and goodness of Yahweh without introducing other beings such as an evil Enlil or Angra Mainyu. The Jews developed their own concept of an adversary who was part of Yahweh's council, answerable to Yahweh, and served as Yahweh's attorney general in confronting humanity. The mythic Hebrew name given to this adversary was hassatan.

We have no clue as to when this hassatan concept was first developed. However, it shows up in only three places in the Hebrew canon, all of which date from the exile and post-exile periods. The three locations are in Job chapters 1–2; Zechariah chapter 3; and 1 Chronicles 21:1, writings which scholars date between 550 to 400 BCE. T. J. Wray and Gregory Mobley list other passages where the term hassatan is used to mean human adversaries but are not translated as "Satan": 1 Samuel 29:4; 2 Samuel 19:22; 1 Kings 5:4 and 11:14; Psalm 109:4.[3]

In Job (500 to 400 BCE), possibly written during the Babylonian exile, we see a legend of testing. It is the most developed role of the mythic hassatan as one of Yahweh's agents to test the integrity of a righteous man. It is Yahweh who invites hassatan, as a cosmic attorney general, to open the file on Job. Wray and Mobley point out that hassatan acts with Yahweh's permission and plays by Yahweh's rules.[4] In Job, hassatan is used primarily to set up the trial in the first two chapters and the mythic name never appears again.

The author of Job brings up two issues: The first is whether the legendary Job, as a symbol for Israel, would love and worship Yahweh as much if all his wealth and comfort were taken away? One by one the fences of protection around Job were taken away and the attorney general (hassatan) is doing everything he can to tempt Job to reject Yahweh. And the trial is on! The three friends restate the Deuteronomic doctrine of retribution: if Job had disobeyed and sinned, the law of justice required him to suffer. Job was experiencing great suffering, therefore, it must be the result of past sins and Yahweh was now punishing him. The response of the three friends, based on the Deuternomic doctrine of retribution is simply to repent and reaffirm

---

3. Wray and Mobley, *Birth of Satan*, 55–58.
4. Ibid., 63.

the established traditions. But in Job, the friend's concept of retribution is rejected.

The University of Michigan professor George Mendenhall sees a second issue. He feels that the book of Job has been widely misunderstood. It is not so much an issue of the theodicy question (why do bad things happen to good people) but one for the future of Israel in which the name Job is really Israel. Why should Israel continue to worship and be loyal to Yahweh if the nation continues to be beaten apart by exiles and other disasters and Yahweh does not come to help? As Mendenhall points out, this was a pressing issue for the leaders in the exile and also for those left in Jerusalem during the exile and post-exile period. The charge is against Yahweh's unreliability. Is he still worthy of worship?[5] This is the same haunting question we saw in Malachi (ca. 500 to 450 BCE). Why should they continue worshiping Yahweh if there is no protection and the unrighteous have no punishment? Maybe Yahweh had simply given up on them as feared in Psalm 77:79:

> Will the Lord spurn forever,
> and never again be favorable?
> Has his steadfast love ceased forever?
> Are his promises at an end for all time?
> Has God forgotten to be gracious?
> Has he in anger shut up his compassion?

In Israel's search for meaning into the future, these are profound questions in Job which hassatan is pressing Israel to answer for itself. With all the chaos Israel was going through, would it be as faithful as the legendary Job? We know the Job story and its ending. Job remains faithful and all is restored. In the end we find that Yahweh does not operate on the justice of law and punishment, but on a justice of love, graciousness, and restoration. The Job legend protects the monotheism of Yahweh by having hassatan as one of Yahweh's agents, not an enemy of Yahweh. Dr. Walter Wink, professor of biblical interpretation at Auburn Theological Seminary, comments that in Job hassatan is not God's enemy but an eager adversary for God prompting profound searching on the part of Israel.[6] In this Job legend, hassatan is one of God's attorney generals, following God's orders, putting Israel to the test. This is not the anti-God Satan of contemporary usage.

The second hassatan passage is Zechariah. Scholars divide his work into two parts: chapters 1–8 (ca. 520 to 518 BCE) and 9–14 (ca. 325 to 300

---

5. Mendenhall, *Ancient Israel's Faith*, 189.
6. Wink, *Unmasking the Powers*, 14.

## Persian Myths and the Introduction of Satan

BCE). Zechariah prophesied in the early days of the Restoration when the returning exiles joined to rebuild their society with those who had never left. Here hassatan speaks for the left-behind peasants who were accusing the high priestly returnees, symbolized by Joshua, of being corrupt and not worthy of Yahweh's support. In Zechariah we read:

> Then he showed me the high priest Joshua standing before the angel of the LORD, and Satan standing at his right hand to accuse him. And the LORD said to Satan, "The LORD rebuke you, O Satan [hassatan]! The LORD who has chosen Jerusalem rebuke you! Is not this man a brand plucked from the fire?" Now Joshua was dressed with filthy clothes as he stood before the angel. The angel said to those who were standing before him, "Take off his filthy clothes." And to him he said, "See, I have taken your guilt away from you, and I will clothe you with festal apparel." And I said, "Let them put a clean turban on his head." So they put a clean turban on his head and clothed him with the apparel; and the angel of the LORD was standing by. (Zech 3:1–5)

To those who were left behind in Jerusalem, Joshua, the high priest, dressed in filthy garments, appears as a symbol for all the wrong deeds of the priests that had caused the Babylonian exile. The term hassatan is used for a functionary of Yahweh's heavenly court acting as a prosecuting attorney accusing Joshua (Israel) of corruption. The popular expectation was that the exiled priests were wicked and guilty, therefore Yahweh would naturally declare Joshua guilty. Yahweh, however, intervenes, reverses the expectation, and takes the guilt away. This story, contrary to popular expectations that sin must eventuate in punishment, illustrates a compassionate, forgiving, and reconciling component of Yahweh, not a punitive one. Hassatan's role is Yahweh's prosecuting attorney bringing the issue to focus. Yahweh gives the surprising final verdict that calls for the restoration of Israel, not its destruction. Hassatan is not demonic here.

The third place where hassatan appears in the Hebrew canon as a proper noun is in 1 Chronicles (ca. 500 to 450 BCE). This is also a post-exile book and a much later rewriting of 2 Samuel. The story is about the reason David took a census. In 2 Samuel 24:1 (written ca. 950 BCE), we read: "And the anger of the Lord was kindled against Israel, and he incited David against them, saying 'Go, count the people of Israel and Judah.'" In this Samuel passage it is the Lord who is requesting the census. Joab and Israel's military commanders protested to David that this was wrong, but the census was taken. A pestilence then came and killed some seventy thousand people. David, believing this was Yahweh's punishment, recognized he had done wrong and repented. Clearly note that this Samuel narrative attributes the census to Yahweh.

In 1 Chronicles 21:1, however, it is the same scene rewritten some five hundred years later. In this later version we must note the cause of the census is hassatan, not Yahweh. "Satan stood up against Israel and incited David to count the people of Israel." This rewriting happened during the same time when the mythic hassatan showed up in Jewish writings, as seen in Zechariah and Job. It appears that the 1 Chronicles passage was written as an editorial attempt to relieve Yahweh of the responsibility for the census and to have the mythic hassatan take the blame.

In these three uses of hassatan, the mythic Satan is working with Yahweh as an adversary, not against Yahweh. Hassatan as an enemy of Yahweh had not yet been developed. It is also significant that the word "devil" never appears in the Hebrew canon and the word "demons" appears only in Deuteronomy 37:17 and Psalm 106:34–38, where they are powers in pagan religions. It is clear that the concept of a devil and demons was not part of Hebrew theology.

## WHAT ABOUT LUCIFER?

The concept of Lucifer comes out of a mistranslation of Isaiah 14. "How you are fallen from heaven, O Day Star, son of Dawn! How you are cut down to the ground, you who laid nations low! You said in your heart, 'I will ascend to heaven. I will raise my throne above the stars of God. . . . I will make myself like the Most High.' But you are brought down to Sheol, to the depths of the Pit" (Isa 14:12–15).

Notice the term "Lucifer" does not appear in this text. It is about a fallen Babylonian king, possibly Helal, son of Shahar, or Nebuchadrezzar, who had persecuted the Israelites and who thought he was god! He is called "Day Star, son of Dawn" in the text. The problems of associating Lucifer with Satan are two. First, Lucifer is a Roman name, not Hebrew. Second, in Roman astronomy Lucifer is the name given to the morning star. Historian and theologian Jerome (ca. 347– 420 CE), in his Bible, mistranslated the Hebrew term "Day Star" into the Roman morning star "Lucifer," which was then picked up in later translations as another name for Satan. Over the centuries this wrongful translation has been misused by poets and other writers to portray a fallen angel that was now called Satan or the Devil.

## CONCLUSIONS

In this chapter we see a questioning of when Yahweh will deliver the Hebrews not only from the exploitation of foreign occupation, but also from the growing corruption and idolatry within the priestly hierarchy. Sharp challenges were raised. Evil was getting so systematically oppressive that only Yahweh could bring about a new heaven and a new earth. It was during this period that hassatan (Satan) first appears as a mythic symbol in Jewish literature. But hassatan is always a mythic name for an adversary or Yahweh's attorney general, not as an enemy of Yahweh. It is important to note that, as yet, there is no Hebrew concept of a hell or of a Satan as defined in our contemporary usage.

# 9

# The Cradle for Apocalyptic Myths

OUR TIME FRAME IS 325 to 60 BCE. Beginning in 325 BCE the Jews will experience occupation by Greek rulers who will bring with them whole new systems of governance, business trade, and their own myths of life and death. In the next four chapters we will take a close look at many critical developments prior to and during this occupation period. In this chapter, it is important to become familiar with the political history of intense chaos, intrigue, and battles, with inter-Greek-Jewish and intra-Jewish fighting that caused serious questioning of Yahweh's protection. Second, in chapter 10, we will look at the Greek myths and the influence which Plato would have brought into Israel during this turbulent period. It will be in these Greek myths where we first find a concept of hell in terms such as hades and Tartarus. Third, in chapter 11, we will watch Israel's search for a new understanding in light of the severe occupation hardships. Malachi's serious question of justice will be pressed concerning the fate of the righteous who die unrewarded and the fate of the unjust who die unpunished. Finally, in chapter 12, we will see the beginnings of Jewish apocalypticism and its mythic gods of Azazel, Mastemah, and Belair as a response to a chaotic period.

The availability of the Dead Sea Scrolls greatly enlarged and enlightened our scholarship for this period. When we examine the politics of this time, we find a picture that is chaotic and anything but politically peaceful. The following history is intricate, full of brutality and inter-group battles. It is essential to walk thoughtfully through it in order to understand the culture in which myths were changed and apocalyptic literature was developed.

In 325 BCE, Alexander the Great's armies swept through the whole Middle East conquering vast territories. Alexander died in 323 BCE and his two major generals, Ptolomey and Seleucius, unable to maintain the unity of the empire, divided various areas between themselves. Lawrence Schiffman, professor of Hebrew and Judaic studies at New York University, describes the times:

> Palestine found itself caught in a tug of war between Ptolemy, ruler of Egypt, and Seleucus, ruler of Syria, until 301 B.C.E. when Ptolemy finally secured his hold on Palestine. . . . During the next 100 years Ptolemaic and Seleucid armies conducted five major battles against each other in Palestine, but the Ptolemies maintained control until 201 B.C.E. when the Seleucids finally defeated them.[1]

## ESTABLISHMENT OF GREEK CITIES

Here I begin to follow closely the excellent scholarship of Victor Tcherikover, professor at the Hebrew University of Jerusalem, in his historic book *Hellenistic Civilization and the Jews*. It was the Greek pattern to establish new cities as a means of assimilating and Hellenizing newly conquered peoples. They did this by promoting Greek schools, theaters, gymnasia, athletic contests, language, literature, and philosophy.

Since the Greeks were polytheists, having a god for almost every occasion and a god for every Greek city, the presence of other religions such as that of the Jews was not initially a problem. In establishing the cities, the Greeks were not trying to change the Hebrew religion. But, they were making drastic changes in their political structures and trying to open Israel to the world around them. For the elite and powerful Jerusalem aristocracy, the appeal of Hellenization was that it would make their nation part of the wider family of nations. There was an eagerness for economic commerce with other nations; a whole new political philosophy and culture which was more like the Greeks.

---

1. Schiffman, *Reclaiming the Dead Sea Scrolls*, 66.

Eliminating Satan and Hell

The all-male gymnasium was not only the center for learning and training, but schooling within it was a prerequisite to becoming a citizen. It was here that Greek myths and Platonic philosophy would have been taught and would have influenced Jewish thought. However, the gymnasium was costly and citizenship became more or less the monopoly of the sons of the wealthy Jews. The peasants and women were not allowed to attend the gymnasium, which left the largest part of the population as powerless noncitizens. But these noncitizen Jews had no intention of abandoning the laws and the Sinai covenant relationship. They were determined to maintain the past and be faithful to Yahweh. The result was a clash that eventually developed, not only between the Jews and the Greeks, but also between the Jewish aristocracy who supported the Hellenistic political reforms and the common people.

## FIGHT OVER THE HIGH PRIESTHOOD

As indicated above, the Ptolemys lost control of Israel in 201 BCE, and it was now under the Syrian Seleucids and their kings, Antiochus III ("the Great," 223 to 187 BCE), Seleucus IV (187 to 175 BCE), and Antiochus IV ("Epiphanes," 175 to 163 BCE). During the Ptolemaic Egyptian period of control of Israel (301 to 201 BCE), the Jewish non-priestly Tobiad family had gained great wealth and had gained powerful political backing. They had ambitions for power and began to control the temple treasury. Tcherikover comments that the temple also served as a deposit bank, giving an added financial basis to the power of the priestly class. "Because the government of Judea was theocratic, the priests who stood at the head of the cult held great secular power. The Temple treasury played the part of a state exchequer. With the power of the Tobiad family the Temple was in danger of becoming the private fund of a few highly placed families that wielded power in the city."[2]

Here began a Jewish struggle for control of the high priesthood during the years of 180 to 167 BCE. Jewish theocracy had placed great power and sacredness into the high priest's office, which for centuries had come only through the Zadok family. However, during this period, two Jewish families, the Zadoks and the Tobiads, began a fight for controlling power. Onaid's Zadock priestly family saw the advantages of Hellenism and

2. Tcherikover, *Hellenistic Civilization*, 155–56.

embraced the Greek political reforms. They also wanted to hold close to the religious laws of Moses and other ancestral laws. They were the noblest and the wealthiest. Against them were the power-seeking non-priestly Jewish family of the Tobiads.

The historicity of the following events is not clearly documented. But the story goes that as long as Zadock Onias was high priest he refused to give up power to the Tobiads. Onias had a brother named Joshua. The Tobiads sought out Joshua and persuaded him to approach King Antiochus to discredit Onias. Joshua then promised Antiochus three hundred talents of silver, and more later, to purchase the high priest position, taking it away from Onias. Now money began to be involved in the politics of the high priesthood as opposed to the historic "call" of Yahweh as determining the high priest. What is clear is that through Joshua, the high priesthood fell under the control of the Tobiads.

## TOBIAD POLITICAL INTRIGUE AND JOSHUA'S NAME CHANGE

Then Joshua changed his name to Jason and received from King Antiochus permission to convert Jerusalem into a Greek *polis* called Antioch. However the Tobiads, not fully trusting Jason to make the religious changes they wanted, plotted to oust Jason from the high priest position and give it to Menelaus who was not of any priestly family. Menelaus' brother, Simon, already held the high position of overseer of the temple. Now the two, Menelaus and Simon, supported by the Tobiads, would control the economics of the temple and the high priesthood. But Jason rebelled and was unwilling to surrender his power to Menelaus.

This began a bitter struggle between the two non-priestly Tobiads: Menelaus was supported by the Tobiad clan against Jason, who was supported by the majority of the people. Soon Jason gained the upper hand, and Menelaus and the Tobiads were forced to escape. Not giving up, Menelaus then proposed to King Antiochus a reform that would abolish the laws of their Jewish fathers, endorse a Greek government, and live according to the laws of the Greek king, rather than the laws of Moses. Menelaus gave Antiochus a sum of money larger than the three hundred talents that Jason had paid for the high priestly position. Now Menelaus, through economic bribery, had purchased the high priest post for himself and compelled Jason to flee to the Land of Ammon (2 Macc 4:25–26).

Since Menelaus had attained power against the will of the population who hated him, he was forced to conduct his rule by means of terror in order to protect himself and his party. To make matters worse, Menelaus won the king's deputy over to his side by bribing him with several gold vessels from the temple. This aroused the common people's anger even more deeply because the temple treasure was the property of all Israel. It was impossible for the people to tolerate the fact that a small group of people were disposing of the vessels as if they owned them. This further infuriated the faithful Jews who were committed to the historic laws of Moses. A popular uprising against Menelaus soon took place. Lysimachus, the brother of Menelaus, armed some three thousand men and a battle took place in the streets of Jerusalem. The people were victorious and Lysimachus was killed.

Jason, the former high priest who had been driven out by Menelaus, wanted to reclaim his position. With a small body of one thousand men he attacked Jerusalem. Menelaus attempted to defend the city but failed and Jerusalem now fell back into Jason's hands. However, 2 Maccabees 5:6 relates that Jason sought to rule the city with a stiff hand and killed a number of citizens who opposed him. Not able to control the outraged citizens, Jason was again forced to flee. Once more, a civil war broke out in Jerusalem with the control passing into the hands of the common people who saw the Hellenizers as destroying the very heart and basis of Judaism.

## THE CIVIL WAR

Now two different Jewish forces confronted one another. On one side were the wealthy Jewish leadership group supporting the political reforms of Hellenization and the abolition of the Jewish religious traditions. On the other side were the somewhat leaderless common people who wanted none of this. Those who remained faithful to the laws of the Torah and the historic traditions saw themselves as the righteous party. The Hellenizing Jewish leaders were now their enemy.

In a once theocratic nation where the high priesthood was seen as the instrument through which the people were represented to Yahweh, and Yahweh was presented to the people, we not only see a corruption of the high priesthood in being sold to the highest bidder, but also a corruption of the temple itself and a battle between fellow Jews. What once began as a struggle for power between the Zadoks and the Tobiads, became a battle between two Tobiad factions (Jason vs. Menelaus). It then became a battle between Menelaus and the common people, and finally, a battle between the common people and Jason again. Where was Yahweh in all this mess? Was there no punishment for the unrighteous leaders? Where was the new heaven and new earth that Isaiah had promised? Was Yahweh powerless in this struggle? Everything seemed to be falling apart.

## ANTIOCHUS EPIPHANES REACTS

The political situation in Jerusalem in 168 BCE became so dangerous it necessitated the personal presence of the Greek Seleucid ruler, Antiochus Epiphanes, to put down the rebellion. On the one hand, the common people were in open rebellion against the Jewish Hellenizers and fighting to preserve the Hebrew faith itself. On the other hand, Antiochus Epiphanes faced a rebellion that could leave him defeated and lose control of the city and the land. He recognized that if it were the religious laws and traditions of the Hebrews which were causing the insurgency, then the laws and religion of the Hebrews had to be destroyed. It is clear Antiochus Epiphanes acted only after the civil war of the Jews left him no choice. And act he did!

Antiochus Epiphanes, "raging inwardly . . . took the city [Jerusalem] by storm. He commanded his soldiers to cut down relentlessly everyone they met and to kill those who went into their houses. Then there was a massacre of young and old, destruction of boys, women, and children, and slaughter of young girls with infants. Within the total of three days eighty thousand were destroyed; forty thousand in hand to hand fighting, and as many were sold unto slavery as were killed" (2 Macc 5:11ff).

Antiochus Epiphanes, believing he had calmed the uprising, left the city in control of loyal governors. According to 2 Maccabees the insurgency broke out again, and again the rebels gained control of Jerusalem. This time,

> in his malice toward the Jewish citizens, Antiochus sent Appolonius, the captain of the Mysians, with an army of twenty-two thousand, and commanded him to kill all grown men and to sell the women and boys as slaves. When this man arrived in Jerusalem, he pretended to be peaceably disposed and waited until the holy sabbath day, then, finding the Jews not at work, he ordered his troops to parade under arms. He put to the sword all those who came out to see them, then rushed into the city with his armed warriors and killed great numbers of people. (2 Macc 5:23–27)

# Eliminating Satan and Hell

Shortly after this, Antiochus Epiphanes sent an Athenian senator into Jerusalem

> to compel the Jews to forsake the laws of their ancestors and no longer to live by the laws of God; also to pollute the temple in Jerusalem and to call it the temple of Olympian Zeus. . . . And the temple was filled with debauchery and reveling by the Gentiles, who dallied with prostitutes and had intercourse with women in the sacred precincts, and besides brought in things for sacrifice that were unfit. The altar was covered with abominable offerings that were forbidden by the laws. People could neither keep the sabbath, nor observe the festivals of their ancestors. (2 Macc 6:1–2, 4–6)

Antiochus Epiphanes then began to settle the city with loyal fellow Syrians. As a result, 1 Maccabees 1:29–30 claims many inhabitants left the city for the wilderness, "they, their sons, and wives and their livestock because of the danger in the city. . . . Jerusalem was uninhabited like a wilderness" (1 Macc 3:4). We can hear the refugees crying, "O Yahweh! Where are you? Can you not act to deliver your covenanted people?"

## THE MACCABEAN REVOLT

Antiochus Epiphanes ultimately outlawed the Jewish religion. Schiffman comments:

> The right to live according to the Torah, granted to the Judeans by Antiochus III, was now rescinded. In its place, the Jews were to live under the law of the Greek city. Jews suddenly found themselves second-class citizens under the oligarchy. . . . Foreign idolatrous worship and cultic prostitution were introduced into the Temple in December 167 BCE. Throughout Palestine, the Sabbath and Festivals were to be violated. Highplaces were built where unclean animals were to be offered. Circumcision was outlawed. The laws of kosher food were not to be observed. The penalty for violating these ordinances was death.[3]

At stake was not simply a religious persecution, but the survival of the Jewish nation. It was to avoid this catastrophe that Judah the Maccabee appeared before the walls of Jerusalem and captured the city. This began a new chapter in the war of liberation.

3. Schiffman, *Reclaiming the Dead Sea Scrolls*, 69–70.

## The Cradle for Apocalyptic Myths

Here let me try to quickly summarize the basic lines of the Maccabean wars. The Syrian general, Apollonius, made his first attempt to suppress the Maccabean rebellion. Judah the Maccabean defeated this attempt and Apollonius was killed. Apollonius was followed by Seron, who was also defeated by Judah the Maccabee. By now the Syrian government of Antiochus Epiphanes realized it had a serious rebellion on its hands. Lysias, who was viceroy to Antiochus Epiphanes, was sent to Judea with a large force under Generals Ptolemy, Nicanor, and Gorgias. This force was also defeated and Judah the Maccabee became master of the entire country of Judea. With Jerusalem recaptured, Judah the Maccabee purified the temple and restored the cult of Yahweh to Israel. This took place some three years after the beginning of the Antiochus' persecution. This first war for independence came to an end in 164 BCE.

However, when Hellenizing the cities of Judah, Antiochus Epiphanes had brought in many settlers from Syria who wanted to continue their own forms of worship. This was not acceptable to the Maccabean insurgents who saw the Syrians as worshiping heathen gods. Now these Syrian-Greeks were the targets of widespread Maccabean attacks and many were slaughtered. In addition to these Syrians, Judah the Maccabee also moved ruthlessly to exterminate the Hellenizing Jews, calling them "criminals" and "transgressors."[4]

Sources in 1 Maccabees 3:8 and 2 Maccabees 8:6 show the civil war had now spread far beyond Jerusalem to the whole of Judea. The people who Judah the Maccabee now hatefully persecuted were the high-born and wealthy Jews, the former rulers of the nation. These were the very people who saw the whole Hellenization process as a way of moving the Jewish backwater sect into an openness to the world. They now stood defenseless before multitudes of insurgents who sought to destroy them. The Hellenizers sought protection from the Syrians and became their loyal confederates. So now there was not only a battle against heathen Syrians in the land, but a civil war by the common people against the aristocratic Jews who had once ruled the country and had controlled the high priesthood and the temple.

What was happening to the peasants, the people of the countryside? Tcherikover relates:

> It is to be assumed that large numbers of people all over the land of Judah had suffered severely from the war without regarding

---

4. Tcherikover, *Hellenistic Civilization*, 212.

themselves as bound to any political party; life on the countryside was unsafe and many of the peasants had left their former abodes and had sought secret asylum in the mountains or had sent their families thither; others had been driven from their lands by the Syrian forces, and perhaps also by the insurgents.... These masses, who had done nothing and were bearing the brunt of the suffering of the civil war without taking part in it, were very dangerous to the authority of the Hellenizers, for these peasants were suffering chiefly from the religious persecution and might easily join the forces of the fighters for freedom.[5]

By the end of 163 BCE, important changes had taken place at Antioch. Antiochus Epiphanes had died and his son, Antiochus V Eupator, ascended the throne. Lysias was now the king's guardian and the supreme ruler of Judah. Lysias lent an attentive ear to the refugee Hellenizers and this time he sent a very large force to put an end once and for all to the rebellion and to reassert Greek Seleucid rule. The beginning was reasonably successful and Judah the Maccabee was compelled to hand over the south Judean fortress of Bet Zur to the Syrians. But the Jews then fortified themselves in Jerusalem to no avail. Lysias again laid siege and captured the city.

Lysias wanted to bring peace to Jerusalem. His first task was to select Alcimus for the post of high priest thinking he would be suitable to both hostile camps and restore the temple. This was to appease the followers of Judas the Maccabee. It did not work. Alcimus "realized that there was no way for him to be safe or have access to the holy altar" (2 Macc 14:3). So he turned for help to Demetrius, son of Seleucus Philopator who had ascended to the Syrian throne. Demetrius sent Alcimus back into Judea with a large Syrian army led by Bacchides. Judah the Maccabee also defeated this new Syrian attack. Demetrius again sent Bacchides back into battle to wreck havoc among the Jews. This time the Syrians won and Judah the Maccabee was killed in 160 BCE.

The Syrians were now in control, but the followers of Judah the Maccabee rallied around Jonathan, his brother, and the civil war blazed up once more. Bacchides, tiring of the war and expenditure of money and men, opened negotiations with Jonathan with an oath to not injure Jonathan for the rest of his life.

5. Ibib., 217.

## THE HASMONEANS

One of the most important results of the Judah the Maccabee wars for Jewish history was the creation of the Hasmonean dynasty that was composed of his followers. For the first time after hundreds of years there had appeared among the Jews an organized military force, a fact that had its repercussions both on the Jewish world and on other peoples. For the next one hundred years the Hasmoneans were the dominant force in Judah and breathed new life into all areas of Jewish culture. However, all was not peaceful and wars continued. The "Hasmoneans did the same as all other monarchs of their time, having drinking parties, taking mistresses in addition to their lawful wives, and persecuting those of their relatives whom they suspected for personal or political reasons."[6]

## CONCLUSIONS

This has been an intricate and painful chapter. We can see why the Jews strongly questioned Yahweh's protection and began a search for a new understanding of what was happening. Had Yahweh abandoned them? Could there be an evil god resisting Yahweh? Can Israeli's enemies ever be punished? In the midst of all this questioning we must also know what the Jews were being taught in the Greek gymnasiums. For this we will look next at the Greek myths of Tartarus, hades, and Plato's concept of hell that would have been introduced during this period to the Jews through the Hellenizing proceses.

---

6. Ibid., 252.

# 10

# Greek Myths of Tartarus and Hades

Our time frame is 325 to 60 BCE. The Greek occupation of Palestine lasted 265 years. As we have seen, it was a time of intense Hellenization and struggle. It was also a time of indoctrinating the Jews into Greek philosophy and myths through the Greek gymnasium schools where there would be taught the terminology of hades and Tartarus. In the early Greek myths, the dead are all sent to hades, there is no initial moral distinction or separation, no punitive quality. The dead do not cease to exist but continue in a shadow-like form called shades. In later Greek mythology there begins to be a moral separation between those who exist without punishment in hades, and the incurably wicked souls who are sent from hades to Tartarus for unending punishment. It is in this mythology that Greek concepts of hell will later appear in Jewish apocalyptic literature.

We also need to recall from chapter 5, Bernstein's careful definition of hell as "a divinely sanctioned place of eternal torment for the wicked. . . . It includes both justice and suffering . . . torment for the wicked which fulfills the requirement that the damned be justly damned—that is, that they deserve their suffering. . . . No neutral land of the dead, however gloomy, can be hell, since hell must punish."[1]

---

1. Bernstein, *Formation of Hell*, 3.

*Greek Myths of Tartarus and Hades*

## GREEK TARTARUS AND HADES

The Eleusinian Mysteries, which go back as far as 1500 BCE were celebrated in major Greek festivals in the Hellenic era. By the time of the Greek occupation of Palestine, the Greeks had developed a sophisticated concept of death. In Hesiod's *Birth of the Gods* (ca. 750 to 650 BCE), creation was divided among Cronos's sons. Zeus took the celestial regions, Poseidon took the seas, with Hades taking the earth and its innards. Here Hades is a mythic person, not a place. However, in Homer's *Hymn to Demeter* (ca. eighth century BCE), we see Hades as a person, but at the same time it is a place of confinement for Persephone and a warehouse for the dead.

Here begins the Greek concept of hades as a temporary storage for the dead located at the very ends of the earth or in the depths of the earth itself. Both the offenders and the righteous are "equal residents in the land of Hades."[2] At this stage it seems that Sheol and hades are somewhat similar. However, in the Greek myth there is a step not in the Hebrew Sheol. In hades each soul had to appear for judgment before Persephone. She would make a decision whether the soul was righteous enough to be rewarded with a return to the Elysian Fields or be sent to punishment in Tartarus. Now we face two things. First was the Greek projection of vengeance against enemies and their punishment after life. Second we meet Tartarus as a very deep underground place of punishment for the incurably wicked. How deep? The Greek writer Hesiod said a bronze anvil falling from heaven would take nine days and nights to reach earth, and an object would take the same amount of time to fall from earth into Tartarus.

But the Hebrew Sheol has a major point of difference from the Greek hades. Sheol has no point of judgment with a judge to either reward the soul to a new life, or condemn it to eternal punishment in Tartarus. As noted earlier, this difference becomes crucial when the Hebrew texts were translated into the Greek Septuagint. The translators chose the Greek word hades for Sheol.

## ORPHISM

The main plot in Greek beliefs of Orphism (sixth century BCE) centered around Zeus, his wife Hara, Persephone, and the Titans. Zeus impregnates Persephone and she has a son, Dionysus. Hara, bitter at Zeus' infidelity,

2. Ibid., 41.

instigates the Titans to murder Dionysus, who had turned himself into a bull. The Titans kill him and eat him. However, Athena saves the heart of Dionysus and informs Zeus. Zeus then directs a thunderbolt at the Titans turning them into soot. In the myth, the human soul is then created from the heart of Dionysus and human flesh is created from the soot of the Titans. Hence the human being is a soul-body dualism, with the soul being divine and immortal, yet being held as a prisoner in an inferior mortal body.

Here begins the early Greek concept of reincarnation where an immortal soul has an independent existence but is held captive until the death of the body. The soul then returns to a cosmic existence, ready to be reincarnated into another body. The more righteous a life is lived during earthly existence, the higher on the ladder will be its reincarnation. In this concept there is not only a clear dualism between the soul and the body but an ethical dualism with reward for righteousness and a penalty for unrighteousness. The measure of righteousness, however, is based upon correct worship of the gods, not on impartial laws. It is also essential for the soul to survive after physical death and be resurrected in order for it to receive judgment in an afterlife of Tartarus.

## PLATO'S RATIONALE FOR HELL

Plato lived between 427 to 347 BCE. In his *Alcibiades I*, we find indications that Plato knew of Zoroaster and Persian religious thought with its influence on the training of young princes:

> And when the young prince is seven years old he is put upon a horse and taken to the riding-masters, and begins to go hunting. And at fourteen years of age he is handed over to the royal schoolmasters, as they are termed: these are four chosen men, reputed to be the best among the Persians of a certain age; and one of them is the wisest, another the justest, a third the most temperate, and a fourth the most valiant. The first instructs him in the magianism of Zoroaster, the son of Oromasus, which is the worship of the Gods, and teaches him also the duties of his royal office.[3]

However, we do not know how much influence Zoroaster had on Plato. While poets and dramatists were reworking the myths, Greek historians and philosophers were beginning to criticize them as no longer legitimate

3. Plato, *Alcibiades I*, 43.

as an adequate explanation of life. They tried to minimize the supernatural as found in such Persian myths of judgment, hell, and their gods of Spenta Mainyu and Angra Mainyu.

As a rationalist, the Greek philosopher Plato greatly expanded Orphic thought and conjectured that perfect forms and ideas exist only in the eternal realm. In Plato's myth of life and death, souls exist immortally in this eternal realm where they experience perfect forms and ideas before taking on human bodies. When the soul takes on a human body, it forgets this eternal knowledge. Therefore, earthly forms and ideas are only partial reflections or recollections of the perfect forms which humans had seen before assuming bodies.

Plato continued the Orphic belief that at birth the immortal soul is imprisoned in mortal flesh that is imperfect. At death the immortal soul is judged. As the historian Bernstein explains:

> When a person dies, the soul leaves the body. It comes to a meadow like the one referred to in the *Gorgias*. There it approaches two pair of openings: one pair conveys those leaving for and returning from the heavens, the other conducts souls leaving for and returning from the interior of the earth. Judges of souls send the unjust downward to the left, scarred by the evidence of all their deeds on their backs. The just are sent upward to the right, marked by a sign of approval.[4]
>
> Every thousand years the souls within the earth are tested as part of their ascent by passing though a mouth-like opening. If the soul is one of incurably wicked or not sufficiently purified, the mouth bellows and the soul is denied return . . . after the alarm sounds and the torment is completed, the demons fling these sinners back into Tartarus. Among those detained are the incurably wicked.[5]
>
> Under the supervision of the Fates, . . . the righteous souls choose lots that give them priority in selecting their next life on earth. Before choosing their new earthly life, they know whether it will involve poverty and virtue or power accompanied by great crimes. They are completely free to choose the life they wish. Once they choose, they will be bound by Necessity to that life.[6]
>
> After each soul has chosen its fate in the next life. Lachesis, a daughter of Necessity, gives to each the genius (daimona) it has

---

4. Bernstein, *Formation of Hell*, 58.
5. Ibid., 59.
6. Ibid.

chosen . . . and a genius leads it to drink from the River Lethe, the river of unmindfulness, whose water obliterates all memory. New lives begin with no memory of the past.[7]

I find no evidence that the Persian concept of a judgment, with its separation of the righteous and the wicked at death, influenced Plato's rationalistic concept of death. However, there are parallel results in Plato's logic of judgment that was based upon three points. One, justice demands punishment for the incurably wicked. Two, if an evil person simply dies and ceases to exist, no punishment is possible and the wicked would escape justice. Three, therefore, the soul must be immortal in order for the evil soul to be resurrected, receive justice, and then punishment after death.

Plato based his logic on a concept of justice that in turn is founded upon a system of laws. If one breaks an established law then the justice system demands the offender be punished. Justice, which if failed to be administered in this life, requires a hell and an afterlife wherein punishment can be given. Since people on earth cannot inflict due punishment on their enemies and others they deem as sinners, the duty is placed on the mythic gods. While good souls are reincarnated back to earth, wicked souls that are also immortal must remain eternally in Tartarus. In Plato's logic this is a justice deserved. But it is another human construct or myth to make sure sinners receive punishment.

The earliest concept of hell we found was in Persian thought where wicked were pushed off the bridge into an eternal hell. Here in Greek thought is the second instance where the incurably wicked, as their punishment, remain eternally in hell without the possibility of earthly reincarnation. Like the powerful Zoroastrian myth, Plato's vision has a complete human cycle with the birth of immortal souls into human bodies, a life of choices, a death with a judgment, a punishment of the wicked and a reward for the righteous. The righteous are reincarnated into human bodies and the cycle begins again. What Plato does not have is a cause for human evil like an Angra Mainyu. He has no Satan. However, Tartarus is the place of eternal punishment and is his mythic hell.

---

7. Ibid., 60.

## CONCLUSIONS

In these Greek myths we see the terms Tartarus and hades being introduced as places of judgment and punishment. We also see the division of the immortal soul from the mortal body, with a resurrection and reincarnation of souls. What is crucial to remember is the Jewish concept of Sheol is decidedly different from the concepts of hades and Tartarus. However, as we have already seen in chapter 5, in the Greek Septuagint translation the Hebrew term for a neutral Sheol unfortunately becomes translated as hades, implying the possibility of eternal punishment in Tartarus.

We are not certain how much influence Persian thought may have had on Greek thinking. We do know, however, that Plato had a powerful influence on his own Greek culture and on the Jews during the Greek occupation. It is no wonder that during this same period, the first of the Jewish apocalypses started to be written about 168 BCE. The Jews had already experienced 130 years of Hellenization, and it will be in 1 Enoch that we find the first Jewish indication of hell. The writer of 1 Enoch may well have chosen his concept of individual judgment and hell from the influence of these Persian and Greek myths. We don't know for sure, but it seems logical.

Two things are clear: One, the concepts of a Hebrew hassatan or Sheol are quite distinct from these Greek myths. Two, Plato's theory is still pure conjecture or myth. It satisfies the vengeance of those who want to make sure their enemies are punished. However, given what we now know about the composition of the earth, none of these Greek myths of a deep underground hades or an even deeper Tartarus would make sense to contemporary scientists.

Next we look at several late Jewish writings coming out of this turbulent period, namely, Isaiah 24–27 and 66, and Daniel 12:2. In these passages we will find possible beginnings of Hebrew resurrection concepts.

# 11

# Search for a Different Understanding

If the scholars' dating of Scripture is correct there are several identifiable biblical passages that were written after Plato and after Malachi between 328 to 167 BCE. These include Third Isaiah 66 and the Little Apocalypse of Second Isaiah 24–27, as well as the book of Daniel. In these works, changing concepts of death begin to emerge.

## THIRD ISAIAH 66 AND GEHENNA

In what scholars feel is a postexilic apocalyptic addition to Third Isaiah, chapter 66 closes with the image of a renewed Israel, a renewed Jerusalem, and the nations coming to Zion (Isa 66:18–23). However, an important word picture is found in Isaiah 66:24. When the worshipers left the temple they could look into what was a burial pit. This location with its continually burning fires was south of Jerusalem and originally called the "valley of the sons of Hinnom" (Hebrew: *g'hennom*). In ancient times it is believed children had been sacrificed though fire in this valley as an offering to the god Molech . . . a practice outlawed by King Josiah (2 Kgs 23:10).

The history of the valley is important to know both for the warnings to the Hebrews, but also for it subsequent use of gehenna in the New Testament gospels. Jeremiah, writing before the 587 BCE exile, comments in two

## Search for a Different Understanding

passages about the Valley of Gehenna, also known as the valley of Topheth. Yahweh tells him to sternly warn the people of Jerusalem.

> For the people of Judah have done evil in my sight, says the LORD; they have set their abominations in the house that is called by my name, defiling it. And they go on building the high place of Topheth, which is in the valley of the son of Hinnom, to burn their sons and their daughters in the fire—which I did not command, nor did it come into my mind. Therefore, the days are surely coming, says the LORD, when it will no more be called Topheth, or the valley of the son of Hinnom, but the valley of Slaughter: for they will bury in Topheth until there is no more room. The corpses of this people will be food for the birds of the air, and for the animals of the earth; and no one will frighten them away. And I will bring to an end the sound of mirth and gladness, the voice of the bride and bridegroom in the cities of Judah and in the streets of Jerusalem; for the land shall become a waste. (Jer 7:30–34)

A similar repeat of this passage is in Jeremiah 19:3–9. These Scriptures are a corporate warning to the "people of Judah" that unless they change they will have a shameful death and end up as corpses in the Valley of Topheth, i.e., in gehenna, as punishment for their disobedience. The normal tradition of the Hebrews was to bury their dead, even criminals and enemy forces, in order to keep the land sacred and free from pollution. In this passage the bodies of Judah will lie disgracefully exposed in the valley and Yahweh says,

> The bones of the kings of Judah, the bones of its officials, the bones of the priests, the bones of the prophets, and the bones of the inhabitants of Jerusalem shall be brought out of their tombs; and they shall be spread before the sun and the moon and all the host of heaven, which they have loved and served, which they have followed, and which they have inquired of and worshiped; and they shall not be gathered or buried; they shall be like dung on the surface of the ground. Death shall be preferred to life by all the remnant that remains of this evil family in all the places where I have driven them, says the LORD of hosts. (Jer 8:1–3)

In these Jeremiah passages we see Yahweh's possible rejection of Judah as severe. Yet, Yahweh never went in the direction to destroy it.

In Third Isaiah 66:24, Jeremiah's warning is recalled. The vivid and sobering word picture of Third Isaiah is that as worshipers leave the temple, they, too, can look into this valley, see the burning, worm infested corpses of those who have rebelled against Yahweh and this will be their lot if they don't change. "And they shall go out and look at the dead bodies of the people who have rebelled against me; for their worm shall not die, their fire shall not be quenched, and they shall be an abhorrence to all flesh" (Isa 66:24).

Two points need to be stressed. First, the Isaiah text in the Hebrew and in the Greek Septuagint versions does not mention gehenna. But according to New Testament scholar Craig Evans, in McDonald and Sander's *Canon Debate*, the first-century Hebrew Targum, which was an interpretive rendering of the passage reads: "will not die and their fire shall not be quenched, and the wicked shall be judged in *Gehenna*."[1] So, clearly Isaiah's warning echoes Jeremiah's same Valley of Gehenna warning. The crucial shift here is that the Targum now connects gehenna to the place of punishment for the wicked in Judah "who have rebelled against God." Later we will see that the Gospel of Mark (9:43–48) appears to be quoting the Targum when it has Jesus using gehenna as a place of punishment.

Second, I want to stress that in both Jeremiah and Isaiah this was a visible, above-ground concept of punishment. This may be the first picture we have of a place with worms and an eternal fire punishing rebellious Judah. But fire needs oxygen to burn, so gehenna cannot be equated with the deep underground Greek myths of hades or Tartarus where there is no oxygen. Sheol was still a place where everyone remained after death even though the bodies of the wicked may have been burnt in gehenna. In the Mishnah, *Sanhedrin* 6:6, it mentions that "when the flesh [of the wicked] had wasted away they gather together the bones and buried them in their own places [i.e., in Sheol]."

Gehenna is not Bernstein's definition of hell nor Zoroastrian and Plato's deep underground place of eternal punishment. However, this concept of gehenna as a place of eternal fire was picked up in 1 Enoch 103, used extensively in the gospels, and is universally translated, or mistranslated as hell. We must look carefully at the gehenna term when we come to 1 Enoch and the gospels.

---

1. McDonald and Sanders, *Canon Debate*, 191–94.

# ISAIAH 24–27, THE LITTLE APOCALYPSE AND RESURRECTION

By the late postexilic stage of Isaiah 66, the Jews had not developed any clear concepts of resurrection. Isaiah chapters 24–27 (ca. 200 BCE) have been called "Isaiah's Little Apocalypse." Scholars have determined that this section of Isaiah was not composed until the occupation period of the Ptolemies with its growing sociopolitical oppression, the corruption of the religious hierarchy, and the influence of Hellenization.

Isaiah chapters 24–27 begin with an oncoming worldwide destruction. The earth lies polluted because the inhabitants have violated the statutes of Yahweh and the historical Sinai covenant. Therefore a curse is about to devour the earth and its inhabitants will suffer for their guilt.

> Now the Lord is about to lay waste the earth and make it desolate,
> and he will twist its surface and scatter its inhabitants. . . .
> The earth shall be utterly laid waste and utterly despoiled;
> for the Lord has spoken this word.
> The earth dries up and withers,
> the world languishes and withers;
> the heavens languish together with the earth.
> The earth lies polluted
> under its inhabitants;
> for they have transgressed laws,
> violated the statutes,
> broken the everlasting covenant.
> Therefore a curse devours the earth,
> and its inhabitants suffer for their guilt;
> therefore the inhabitants of the earth dwindled,
> and few people are left. (Isa 24:1–6)

There will be a day of judgment of both the deities in heaven and the kings of the earth and they will be punished (Isa 24:21–22). It will come upon all people; the powerful and the weak, the rich and the poor, without regard for their social or ethical standing. This is not about the suffering of the Jews alone. The whole earth is devoured by a systemic evil. Yet, even with this picture of doom, the writer expresses confidence in the sovereignty and power of Yahweh to bring about peace for all peoples and nations.

> On this mountain the Lord of hosts will make for all peoples
> a feast of rich food, a feast of well-matured wines,

> of rich food filled with marrow, of well-matured wines strained clear.
> And he will destroy on this mountain
> the shroud that is cast over all peoples,
> the sheet that is spread over all nations;
> he will swallow up death for ever.
> Then the Lord God will wipe away the tears from all faces,
> and the disgrace of his people he will take away from all the earth,
> for the Lord has spoken.
> It will be said on that day,
> Lo, this is our God; we have waited for him, so that he might save us.
> This is the Lord for whom we have waited;
> let us be glad and rejoice in his salvation.
> For the hand of the Lord will rest on this mountain. (Isa 25:6–10)

In these chapters there is a vision of Yahweh's restoration of both the people and the earth, and even the elimination of death (Isa 25:7). The suffering which the innocent have endured and the blood of the righteous which had been spilled will be avenged. We find this in two contrasting passages of Isaiah 26. The first passage: "O Lord our God, other lords besides you have ruled over us, but we acknowledge your name alone. The dead do not live; shades [corpses] do not rise—because you have punished and destroyed them, and wiped out all memory of them" (Isa 26:13–14). The image in this passage is one where all of Israel's enemies have been destroyed and are in Sheol from whence their dead cannot rise again. In these two chapters, 25 and 26, God's name will be restored on earth, death will be swallowed up forever, the paths of righteousness will be made smooth.

The second passage is Isaiah 26:19. In contrast to above, God has restored Israel to glory with a concept that faithful Israelites who have already died will be resurrected and restored. "Your dead shall live, their corpses shall rise. O dwellers in the dust, awake and sing for joy! For your dew is a radiant dew, and the earth will give birth to those long dead" (Isa 26:19). Here appears be the first Jewish expression of a resurrection. However, there is no clear picture of where the "just" are to be located except that they will rise.

The issue here is whether this is part of an individual's prayer to Yahweh and refers to a developing belief in a resurrection of faithful individuals. Or, is Yahweh speaking to the whole Jewish community, reassuring it that Yahweh will resurrect the whole nation to a new creation as in chapter 65:17? If it is the latter, it is consistent with the entire message of Isaiah where Yahweh will do what human leadership cannot do in the face of systemic evil. Namely, create a new heaven and a new earth that we have already examined.

> For I am about to create new heavens and a new earth; the former things shall not be remembered or come to mind. But be glad and rejoice forever in what I am creating for I am about to create Jerusalem as a joy, and its people as a delight. I will rejoice in Jerusalem, and delight in my people; no more shall the sound of weeping be heard in it, or the cry of distress. (Isa 65:17–18)

In these last four chapters we consistently see the sovereignty of God over a rebellious people. Here, the writer's confidence is based on a gracious Yahweh who will destroy evil and restore Israel as a fruitful garden on earth. The scattered Jews will return to Jerusalem from all nations.

> On that day the Lord will thresh from the channel of the Euphrates to the Wadi of Egypt, and you will be gathered one by one, O people of Israel. And on that day a great trumpet will be blown, and those who were lost in the land of Assyria and those who were driven out to the land of Egypt will come and worship the Lord on the holy mountain at Jerusalem. (Isa 27:12–13)

The destruction is a future threat. But Yahweh is restorative, not punitive. There is no Satan in these few chapters. Yahweh's justice is executed on a judgment day, but there is no burning hell. The new elements are the possibility of a moral death, a division between the just and unjust, and a possible resurrection of the righteous dead.

## DANIEL 12

The only other Old Testament passage in which we find a resurrection concept is in Daniel 12. This passage was written ca. 167 BCE during Antiochus and the Jewish revolts. "There shall be a time of anguish, such as has never occurred since nations first came into existence. But at that time your people shall be delivered, everyone who is found written in the book. Many of those who sleep in the dust of the earth shall awake, some to everlasting life, and some to shame and everlasting contempt" (Dan 12:1b–2).

In this passage, we see a second indication of a distinct resurrection of humanity. The just will be resurrected to everlasting life, but the unjust resurrected to shame and everlasting contempt. However, in this Daniel

## Eliminating Satan and Hell

passage there is no location designated for those who awake to everlasting life or for those who suffer everlasting shame and contempt. No Tartarus, or hades, or gehenna is mentioned.

What seems to be clear is that a vague concept of resurrection appears only in later stages of Hebrew writings. The concept arises in the Persian and Platonic logic that the just who suffered in life should be rewarded and resurrected. The unjust who did not suffer in this life should receive eternal punishment in a hell. Such after-death reward or punishment would require a resurrection. Any Jewish support for the Persian or Greek logic seems to be very tentative. Certainly not everyone agreed. In the sectarian communities that developed after the Maccabean wars only the Pharisees embraced a resurrection concept.

### THE GREEK SEPTUAGINT TRANSLATION

It is important for our study to understand, again, the nature of the manuscripts during this period. Because Jews were widely dispersed around the Greek empire, the text of the Hebrew Masoritic Bible was translated into Greek around 285 to 247 BCE. This Greek Septuagint translation was used primarily by Hellenistic Jews but not by Palestinian Jews. One major negative factor as a result of the translation from the Hebrew to the Greek, as we have noted before, is that Sheol, as a place of nothingness, was translated into the Greek as hades, which implies the historic Greek meaning of Plato's hades and a step toward punishment for the incurably wicked. This radically changed the meaning of Sheol into hades.

Another interesting factor in the Septuagint was that Daniel, originally placed in the Writings (the Ketuvim) in the Masoritic text, was later moved to the section of the Prophets. This allowed a change in the focus of Daniel from being a book to encourage the Hebrews to maintain faith in Yahweh during the Antiochus-Maccabean wars, to a view of Daniel as a book prophesying the coming of a "messianic person" in the form of the "son of man coming on the clouds of angels," i.e., Jesus. This was a distortion of Daniel. Since New Testament writers often used the Septuagint to seek passages that could be read as predicting the birth of Jesus, the Jews felt this was a misuse of their Scriptures. Therefore, once the Septuagint was adopted by Christianity its importance for the Jews soon evaporated. It was replaced by other Jewish translations into Greek that adhered more closely to the Masoritic text.

*Search for a Different Understanding*

## THE APOCRAPHA AND PSEUDEPIGRAPHA

It was during this same historical period that two classes of manuscripts were being written. The first class of literature is the Apocrypha that includes fourteen manuscripts written between 250 BCE and about 6 BCE. These were never included in the Hebrew Masoritic Scriptures as the Apocrypha texts were not deemed, as Lawrence Schiffman indicates, "to constitute the authorized record of God's revelation, direct or indirect, to humanity."[2] However, with the exception of 2 Esdras, all were added to the Septuagint. These Apocryphal texts were also included in Roman Catholic and Eastern Orthodox Bibles, but not in Protestant Bibles.

The second class of manuscripts were called the Pseudepigrapha because their writers were pseudonymous authors who used the names of ancient heroes for their book titles to give importance to them. It is in the Pseudeprigraphic literature where we see the apocalyptic tangent taking off most clearly. However, no Pseudepigrapha texts were included in the Hebrew Masoritic Bible or the Septuagint.

## CONCLUSIONS

It was during the period of Greek chaos and oppression where we saw the Jews searching for a new understanding of Yahweh, of death and of evil. *Gehenna* became a significant term as a place of punishment. A vague concept of resurrection begins to emerge either for the nation itself or for righteous individuals. Is this development a combination of (a) the Jewish disappointment that the messiah had not come, (b) the influence of Persian thought about punishing gods, and (c) Plato's dualism, reincarnation and a place of eternal punishment for wicked immortal souls, all combined together? There is no clear narrative to support this, but it is a logical progression of thought when searching for answers. Finally, we must recognize the importance of the Septuagint's mistranslating a non-punishing Sheol into a hades as a step toward punishment.

I turn next to the Jewish apocalyptic myths in 1 Enoch, Jubilees and the Sibyllene Oracles, each found in the Pseudepigrapha. In these books we will see significant shifts in Jewish mythical thinking.

---

2. Schiffman, *Reclaiming the Dead Sea Scrolls*, 161.

# 12

# Jewish Apocalyptic Myths

THE APOCALYPTIC TIME FRAME is 250 to 165 BCE. The situation which many Jews faced seventy-five years following the exile was one in which the established patterns did not bring a new heaven on earth. The role of kingship had been discredited. Ezekiel's kingship of Yahweh, with the centralization of everything in the temple and its dominating priesthood, was not working. The temple system had returned to corruption and idolatry. The Jewish hierarchy's support for and dependency upon Persian and later Greek powers only brought more misery and oppression. The whole of society's institutions and structures were viewed as embodying new systems of political, social and economic evil that transcended any individual's sin. Isaiah 59:14–15 expresses the broken culture they were experiencing:

> Justice is turned back,
> and righteousness stands at a distance;
> for truth stumbles in the public square,
> and uprightness cannot enter.
> Truth is lacking,
> and whoever turns from evil is despoiled.

We have already seen when myths no longer work there is a search for a new understanding. This was now happening in the postexilic period of Jewish history. Apocalyptic eschatology was the shift to find new answers to why the messiah had not come. The theodicy question of why evil was urgently pressed for an answer. If Yahweh is all-powerful and all good, why is this happening to the very people whom Yahweh has called "my chosen"?

## Jewish Apocalyptic Myths

And Malachi's question of why the wicked were not getting punished in this life was still not answered.

The answers were really only three. One could blame Yahweh. We saw in chapter 6 that Second Isaiah placed a heavy burden on Yahweh as the One and only God who was the author of both good and evil. But if one wants to protect the integrity and monotheism of Yahweh as not being able to do evil, then the options were reduced to two. One could blame human freedom of choice as we have seen in past Jewish literature. Or, one could blame an evil sub-god like an Enlil or a Angru Mainyu. It would be understandable for Jewish thinkers, being exposed to Persian and Greek mythology, to question past answers and begin reworking their theology.

There are no definitive smoking guns connecting Jewish apocalyptic myths to prior Persian and Greek mythologies. However it was in this historical period of apocalyptic writings where the mythical hassatan, earlier one of Yahweh's agents, shifted to Azazel in Enoch and to Belial and Mastemah in Jubilees. Now each: Satan, Azazel, Belial, and Mastemah, became mythic names for a "systemic evil" that was far deeper than individual sin and which had infected humanity. It was also during this same historical period when the neutral death of Sheol shifted into defined mythical locations of glory for the righteous and eternal punishment for the wicked. We also get a place of punishment for those deemed as enemies and/or sinners. We need to follow these shifts in the apocalyptic literature we will be examining. Auburn Theological Seminary professor Walter Wink reminds us that the question of evil had

> obsessed Jewish writers from the time of the exile. Israel's misfortunes were too great to ascribe purely to human sin. Adam and Eve could not bear the weight of all human tragedy. The ancient myth of the fall of the "sons of God" in Genesis 6:1–4 was enlisted to explain the presence of evil that emanates not from humanity alone but from something higher as well, not divine, but transcendent, suprahuman, that persists through time, is opposed to God and human faithfulness, and seeks our destruction, damnation, illness, and death. The fall, mischief, and judgment of the angels is one of the chief preoccupations of intertestamental Jewish literature, it's most striking innovations and most lasting contributions to theodicy.[1]

---

1. Wink, *Naming the Powers*, 23.

## 1 ENOCH

First Enoch is what Paul Hanson deals with in his book *The Dawn of the Apocalyptic*. It is a mythical and apocalyptic text of visionary stories that was placed in the Pseudepigrapha and never accepted as scriptural by the Hebrews. The writer of 1 Enoch chose the pseudegraphic name of Enoch since Genesis 5:24 reads: "Enoch walked with God; then he was no more, because God took him." The book begins by assuming that since Enoch was now in the presence of God he would also know the secrets of God. This claim gave legitimacy to the mythic legend of Enoch.

It is also important to recognize that various parts of 1 Enoch were composed over a long span time (ca. 300–50 BCE) and is divided into five sub-books. This fact alone indicates there were multiple legends by differing writers which may give somewhat accurate accounts of what the people were experiencing, but their cosmic descriptions of hell are clearly mythic and not to be taken literally. Key for us will be books 1, 5 and 2.

- Book 1, chapters 1–36, Book of Watchers, ca. 250–225 BCE.
- Book 2, chapters 37–71, Book of Parables (Similitudes), perhaps as late as 50 BCE.
- Book 3, chapters 72–82, Book of Luminaries, ca. 300–250 BCE.
- Book 4, chapters 83–90, Book of Dreams, ca. 168 BCE.
- Book 5, chapters 91–108, Epistle of Enoch, ca. 168 BCE; within this epistle, the Apocalypse of Weeks.

### BOOK 1: SYSTEMIC EVIL SHIFTED TO AZAZEL

In the midst of the Greek occupation and the Jewish civil wars, the writer speaks with fury against the whole corrupt system. Tcherikover uses summary comments from the Ethiopian Enoch to describe it.

> The wealthy who accumulate their wealth unrighteously, who oppress the poor and persecute the just (85:7; 86:8; 87:8–10); they trust in their riches, but their trust is in vain, for they are doomed to destruction on the day of judgment and God himself will rejoice at the fall of the wealthy (84:7–8; *ib.* 10). The evil mock the righteous, but on judgment day the just will ascend to heaven, while the evil will go down to hell (103:1ff.; 100:1ff.). God will wreak havoc among the wicked, and the righteous too will take part in

the vengeance, and slaughter their persecutors ruthlessly (88:12). The wealthy are also the evil and the "unbelievers." They transgress the laws of the Torah of Moses (89:2), and the author of this section has no hesitation in accusing his foes of actual idolatry. (89:9; ib. 14).[2]

The author of 1 Enoch sees all about him the dehumanizing instruments of power and the greed of consumption until the peasants, as victims, were unable to keep up supply. There was open transgression of the Torah and the whole political-economic-religious system was seen to be full of evil. It is crucial to understand how hard it was for them to conceptualize such systematic evil. Apocalyptic writers tried to do it by giving it mythic names such as Azazel and Satan. These mythic names were their shorthand way of describing and helping people come to grips with this overpowering disease of evil. The gods and their names were mythic, but the earthly systems of evil they were experiencing were real.

Book 1 reaches back into Genesis 6 and the myth of the Watchers to find responses to the question of evil. In Enoch we meet Azazel, one the Watchers in Genesis 6, who was named as the personification of evil and the chief fomenter of corruption on earth.

> Asael (Azazel) taught men to make swords of iron and weapons and shields and breastplates and every instrument of war. He showed them metals of the earth and how they should work gold to fashion it suitably, and concerning silver, to fashion it for bracelets and ornaments for women. And he showed them concerning antimony and eye paint and all manner of precious stones and dyes. . . . And the giants began to kill men and to devour them. And they began to sin against the birds and beasts and creeping things and the fish, and to devour one another's flesh. And they drank the blood. Then the earth brought accusation against the lawless ones. (Book 1, 7:3–6)

In Enoch book 1, what I will call "systemic evil" was given the name of Azazel as an out of control Watcher wrecking havoc on earth. Here is where we find a reaching back to the pre-monotheistic evil spirit of the desert as the anti-god who corrupts systems within Yahweh's creation. Azazel becomes the cause of, and also the name for, this systemic evil which is hostile to God and humanity. This is a major shift away from the Hebrew concept of hassatan as Yahweh's attorney general.

2. Tcherikover, *Hellenistic Civilization*, 258–59.

## Eliminating Satan and Hell

Who were the victims of this evil system now named Azazel? They were the lowerclass masses, especially the peasants who generated the labor and goods for the wealth and power of the political and religious elite. In reality, however, everyone was entangled in supporting a system of evil, both the exploiter and the exploited. While oppression comes from the Greek occupiers and the Jewish hierarchy, the common people and the peasants were also coconspirators and all were entrapped together in systemic evil to accumulate wealth and maintain the power of the elite.

At this point, book 1 foretells a needed destruction of everything on earth by repeating the Noah flood legend with the projection that "The Most High" will destroy everything. "Go to Noah and say to him in my name, 'Hide yourself.' And reveal to him that the end is coming, that whole earth will perish; and tell him that a deluge is about to come on the whole earth and destroy everything on the earth" (Book 1, 10:2–3). Here, again we see the human vengeance theme of wanting to destroy everything that has been causing pain and start a new earthly creation re-creating the garden of Eden.

At another point, however, the righteous will escape judgment. They will live until they beget thousands, and all the days of their youth and their old age will be completed in peace. "Then all the earth will be tilled in righteousness, and all of it will be planted with trees and filled with blessing; and all the trees of joy will be planted on it. . . . And all the sons of men will become righteous, and all the peoples will worship God. "All the earth will be cleansed from all defilement and from all uncleanness, and I shall not again send upon them any wrath or scourge for all the generations of eternity" (Book 1, 10:18, 21–22). In spite of the author's picture of Israel under Greek control and with all areas of Jewish life experiencing systemic evil, in the end Yahweh will not destroy but will restore humanity. Azazel, as the mythic symbol of all systemic evil, will be destroyed.

What happens to the dead, especially to the wicked? In book 1, Enoch is led to the middle of the earth where there were three locations to separate the spirits of the dead. One location is for the righteous dead who are located in the earth, one for sinners not having been punished on earth, and one for sinners who were godless and companions of the lawless (22:9–13). Here all are in Sheol. But now Sheol is no longer conceived as a neutral place. Rather it became a place of gradations and separations for sinners each of whom will be appropriately punished by the gods. Book 1 answers Malachi's question with an affirmation that sinners will be punished by the

*Jewish Apocalyptic Myths*

gods who will use methods of unending cruelty which humans could not inflict. In essence, counter-evil will be used to punish evil.

## BOOK 5: SHEOL AND THE PUNISHMENT OF THE WICKED

Book 5 was written during the chaotic Jewish revolt and Antiochus Epiphanes' persecution of 168 BCE, some eighty to ninety years later than book 1. Here we see a sharper punishment of the wicked, who in the end will suffer judgment, distress, and now fire.

> Woe to you, dead sinners. When you die in your sinful wealth, those who are like you say about you, "Blessed are the sinners all their days that they have seen. And now they have died with goods and wealth, and affliction and murder they have not seen in their life. They have died in splendor, and judgment was not executed on them in their life." Know that down to *Sheol* they will lead your souls, and there they will be in great distress, and in the darkness and in a snare and in a flaming fire. Into great judgment your souls will enter, and the great judgment will be for all generations of eternity. Woe to you, you will have no peace. (Book 5, 103:3–8)

We see again the shift in the meaning of Sheol from a neutral place of death with no reward or punishment. Here the dead sinners are in the Sheol we saw in book 1. However, in this book 5, Jewish apocalyptic thought has shifted to where it has taken the above-ground fires in the Valley of Gehenna of Isaiah 66:24, along with the original myth of Sheol, and combined them with the deep underground Greek myth of Tartarus. Since Tartarus is mentioned in 1 Enoch (20:1), this passage completes this shift. We must note that this is clearly mythical because as we have already seen in examining gehenna, underground locations cannot have fire because there is no oxygen.

It is not until books 1 and 5 that we find the first clear concept of individual judgment and a mythical hell in Jewish apocalyptic literature. As mentioned earlier, the first indication of such in Greek literature was in Plato. After 140 years of Hellenization during the Greek occupation, can there be any other place to look than Greek mythology and thought for influence on Enoch? The chaos and suffering of systemic evil was now so intense that a neutral Sheol no longer worked. A sense of justice required punishment by Azazel of evildoers. Sheol has now shifted to be that mythical place for punishment with gehenna's eternal fire.

But, again, we must be clear that this is pure conjecture, pure myth, on the part of the apocalyptic writers of 1 Enoch to explain their world and a justification for a needed punishment of those who were oppressing them during this painful period. This mythic description is picked up in the gospels, especially in Matthew 13:42, 50; 18:8–9; and 25:41.

## BOOK 2: AZAZEL AND SON OF MAN

Book 2 reflects a continued painful situation of 175 years later than book 1, and 125 years later than book 5. This is a period after the Jewish civil war, after Antiochus, after the Maccabean Revolt, after the Hasmonean period and maybe ten years into the Roman period of occupation, all of which are historical periods of Jewish distress. In book 2, written as late as 50 BCE, the term Satan finally shows up. In the Valley of Punishment Enoch asks: "For I saw all the angels of punishment dwelling there and preparing all the instruments of Satan. And I asked the angel of peace who went with me. 'These instruments—for who are they preparing them?' And he said to me, 'They are preparing these for the kings and the mighty of this earth, that they may perish thereby'" (bk. 2, 53:3–5).

Satan's role here is not clear. If anything the instruments of Satan will be used against kings and the mighty of the earth that they may perish. Is it Azazel who will use the instruments of Satan against humans? Is the Satan term still an agent of Yahweh or has Satan become a compliant agent of Azazel? Or are the two are working together in book 2 as symbols of systemic evil? It appears that they are working together, thus making both Azazel and Satan mythic figures of speech representing an evil infection that has plagued every aspect of Jewish life so thoroughly that only Yahweh can intervene to heal it.

Book 2 also has a "son of man" as a Messianic figure, the "Chosen One" who existed before all creation. This messianic figure is the one who will enter into humanity, destroy systemic evil, and recreate an ideal garden of Eden.

> On that day, I shall make my Chosen One dwell among them and
> I shall transform heaven and make it a blessing and a light forever;
> and I shall transform the earth and make it a blessing. (Book 2, 45:4–5)
> And this son of man whom you have seen—he will raise the kings and the mighty from their couches, and the strong from

their thrones. He will loosen the reins of the strong, and he will crush the teeth of the sinners. He will overturn the kings from their thrones and their kingdoms, because they do not exalt him or praise him, or humbly acknowledge whence the kingdom was given to them. (Book 2, 46:4-5)

And in that hour that son of man was named in the presence of the Lord of Spirits, and his name, before the Head of Days. Even before the sun and the constellations were created, before the stars of heaven were made, his name was named before the Lord of Spirits. (Book 2, 48:2-3)

For the Chosen One has taken his stand in the presence of the Lord of Spirits; and his glory is forever and ever, and his might, to all generations. And in him dwell the spirit of wisdom and the spirit of insight, and the spirit of instruction and might and the spirit of those who have fallen asleep in righteousness. And he will judge the things that are secret, and a lying word none will be able to speak in his presence; For he is the Chosen One in the presence of the Lord of Spirits according to his good pleasure. (Book 2, 49:2b-4)

Since humanity can no longer correct itself, Yahweh must act through the Son of Man. This is Enoch's only hope for the future. These concepts of the "Chosen One," the "Son of Man," "before the world was created," "the spirit of wisdom and insight," etc. are all terms that New Testament writers will relate to Jesus. Enoch's basic message is to not fear when sinners seem to be the winners. If you are not a companion of evil, you will be a companion of the host of heaven (book 5, 104:1-6). In a new understanding of Sheol, the sinners will be destroyed with eternal fire. Azazel (systemic evil) will eventually be destroyed and the Son of Man will bring about a new sinless earth.

To review: 1 Enoch is an apocalypse. It makes no pretense to be anything but a mythic attempt at that time in history to make sense out of all the persecution and dehumanization the Jews were suffering. It makes full use of apocalyptic symbols and mythic characters. Yahweh is still in control and will bring about a new creation, a new shalom. The unrighteous, both weak and mighty, will see a judgment day which gives hope to the readers for justice and punishment for their enemies.

For the first time we see significant shifts in the meaning of Sheol and the use of Azazel and Satan as mythic names for systemic evil that are hostile to God and destroys the Sinai covenant relationship between human and God. We see full justice carried out, not by the hands of humans nor even of Yahweh, but by the "angels of punishment" who will be the punishers. But we must emphasize that 1 Enoch was rejected as part of the authoritative record of God's revelation and thus was never included in the Hebrew canon nor the Apocrypha.

## THE SIBYLLINE ORACLES: TARTARUS AND GEHENNA

While in 1 Enoch there were further shifts in the meanings of both Sheol and hassantan, in the Sybilline Oracles (ca. 200–100 BCE) we find a joining of the Greek Tartarus and the Jewish gehenna. The original Oracles were a collection of Roman heathen mythology that was lost in a great fire in 83 BCE. This sparked an attempt in 76 BCE to recollect them when the Roman senate sent envoys throughout the world to discover copies. Current scholars consider the book's original version to be completely Jewish in origin with some later elements of Christian revision.

The Oracles book 5 in which we find gehenna mentioned, is considered to be among the oldest of oracles which would place it between 200 to 100 BCE during the time of intense Jewish fighting and suffering. The text in question is book 5, verses 208–248. Verses of 208–220 proclaim that God will not destroy those who repent and seek pardon. It is verses 221–248 that depict an end time of fire and destruction. Here we find a significant conjoining of Tartarus and gehenna.

> There shall be over all the world a fire
> And greatest omen with sword and with trump
> At sunrise; the whole world shall hear the roar
> And mighty sound. And he shall burn all earth,
> And destroy the whole race of men, and all
> The cities and the rivers and the sea;
> All things he'll burn, and it shall be black dust.
> But when now all things shall have been reduced
> To dust and ashes, and God shall have calmed
> The fire unspeakable which he lit up,
> The bones and ashes of men God himself
> Again will fashion, and he will again
> Raise mortals up, even as they were before.
> And then shall be the judgment, at which God
> Himself as judge shall judge the world again;
> And all who sinned with impious hearts, even them,
> Shall he again hide under mounds of earth

[Dark Tartarus and Stygian Gehenna].
But all who shall be pious shall again
Live on the earth [and (shall inherit there)
The great immortal God's unwasting bliss,]
God giving spirit life and joy to them
[The pious; and they all shall see themselves
Beholding the sun's sweet and cheering light.
O happy on the earth shall be that man].[3]

The image here is one where God will burn the whole earth and everything in it to dust. Then God will take the bones and ashes to renew pious humans on earth as they were before. But those who sinned will be buried below in mounds in "Dark Tartarus and Stygian Gehenna." Here is the first joining of Tartarus and gehenna I have found. If so, the writer takes the mythic Greek Tartarus concept of a very deep and vast underground storehouse of sinners being punished eternally, and imposes its meaning on gehenna. Which as we have seen is the above ground and visible Jerusalem garbage valley outside the city. If this is correct, the Sibyl totally changes the meaning of gehenna. We noted earlier that in developing the Septuagint the translators translated the word Sheol as the Greek hades. In the Sibylline Oracle we now see the mythic Tartarus and the non-mythic gehenna concepts joined as the place of punishment. This conjoining becomes the mythical place for evil people who were not punished during their lifetimes. Again, we must emphasize that the Jews rejected the Sibylline Oracles as part of their Scriptures.

## JUBILEES: LAW AND RETRIBUTION

Jubilees (ca. 175 BCE) is a rewriting of Genesis and Exodus 1–14. Since there is no mention of the Antiochus-Maccabean wars, it is probably written during the Hellenistic reforms prior to 168 BCE. The author was likely a Palestinian Jew from a priestly family. Schiffman writes that Jubilees

> presents itself as a sort of alternative to the canonical Torah, a supposedly more accurate picture of the true divine revelation. Obedience to this Torah will bring the End of Days. A constant theme informing the additions to the book is Jewish law. The author attempts throughout to claim that the patriarchs and other heroes

---

3. Wikipedia, s.v. "Sibylline Oracles."

### Eliminating Satan and Hell

of Genesis observed all the laws to be given at Sinai, especially the ritual calendar of Festivals. The author inserts numerous points of Jewish law into the patriarchal narrative where they do not appear in the canonical Torah.[4]

The book begins its narrative with Moses on Mt. Sinai and an angel commanding Moses to write down all that God commands. The Israelites' failure in Jubilees will center on their neglect of the law, especially the laws of the festivals, the sabbath, the tabernacle, and the sanctuary.

> And many will perish and they will be taken captive, and will fall into the hands of the enemy, because they have forsaken my ordinances and my commandments, and the festivals of my covenant, and my sabbaths, and my holy place which I have hallowed for myself in their midst, my tabernacle, and My sanctuary, which I have hallowed for myself in the midst of the land, that I should set my name upon it, and that it should dwell there. (Jub 1:9)

Jubilees frames its most important theme around the law and retribution. It is clear the writer of Jubilees felt the historical disasters would not have happened had the Hebrew fathers obeyed the commandments. To keep disaster from happening again, a strict obedience will be required and then, maybe, Yahweh will relent and redeem Israel. If such obedience is embraced, Yahweh will embrace them.

> And after this they will turn to Me from amongst the Gentiles with all their heart and with all their soul and with all their strength, and I will gather them from amongst all the Gentiles, and they will seek me, so that I shall be found of them, when they seek me with all their heart and with all their soul.... And I will build My sanctuary in their midst, and I will dwell with them, and I will be their God and they shall be My people in truth and righteousness. And I will not forsake them nor fail them; for I am the Lord their God. (Jub 1:14, 16–17)

Again, in this passage we continue to see the long-held conviction that God will not give up on the Jews, but will reclaim and restore them.

---

4. Schiffman, *Reclaiming the Dead Sea Scrolls*, 186.

## OTHER JUBILEES ISSUES: SHEOL, SATAN, MASTEMAH, BELAIR

There is also a flood story in Jubilees following the Genesis chapter 6 pattern, clearly blaming the flood on the Watchers. "And the Lord destroyed everything from off the face of the earth; because of the wickedness of their [Watchers] deeds, and because of the blood which they had shed in the midst of the earth, He destroyed everything." (Jub 5:25)

However, the Sheol of Jubilees follows the classic Hebrew concept we have seen before rather than the apocalyptic concept. "And there shall not be left any man that eateth blood, or that sheddeth the blood of man on the earth, Nor shall there be left to him any seed or descendants living under heaven; For into *Sheol* shall they go, And into the place of condemnation shall they descend, And into the darkness of the deep shall they all be removed by a violent death." (Jub 7:29)

We see a violent death as the final punishment. But, there is no resurrection or an eternal punishment in hell in Jubilees. What is new is a mixture of personal names for the evil one. Mastemah (meaning "animosity, enmity or hatred") is the chief of evil spirits. It is he who is aggressively evil, contrary to Yahweh, and pushing humans to greater sin. It is Mastemah, who, when all the evil spirits were "bound in the place of condemnation," challenged Yahweh to allow a tenth of them to remain on earth. When Yahweh allows this, these remaining spirits were then placed under Mastemah's command and they spread evil upon the land (Jub 11:4). The name Belair (or Belial, meaning "without value") is also used as the tempter and accuser. We will see this figure used in the Qumran community. Again, we must be clear that these mythic names are figures of speech personalizing systemic evil similar to what we saw in 1 Enoch.

## CONCLUSIONS

This has been a complex chapter with shifting concepts developing. We must continue to recognize we are still dealing with mythic concepts that try to explain what was happening to the Jews. It is only in apocalyptic texts such as 1 Enoch, the Sibylline Oracles, and Jubilees where we have seen major shifts into personalized figures of evil as Azazel, Satan, Belial, and Mastemah. It is also where we first see Sheol used as afterlife place of punishment conjoined with the Greek Tartarus.

## Eliminating Satan and Hell

Out of these writings we see an apocalyptic theology, born out of suffering and despair, seeking answers by reaching back into ancient myths to explain systemic evil. It was during this period we see writings that try to answer why the wicked are not punished and the development of revenge and violence being carried out after death in regions of hell. We also see hassatan no longer as one of Yahweh's attorney generals, but now as Yahweh's enemy. These myths were still being reworked in this cradle of chaotic history. But such apocalyptic books as 1 Enoch, the Sibylline Oracles, and Jubilees, were never included in the Hebrew canon as part of the authorized record of God's revelation.

Maybe another word needs to be said here. The term "authorized" does not carry the same meaning as "inerrant" or "infallible." The Jews knew there had been too many streams of writing and revisions to carry the weight of infallibility. Concepts of infallibility and inerrancy do not come into play until the second Christian century and even more firmly in the time of Copenicus (1473 to 1543 CE). It was than that some theologians denied the new science of the planets inerrantly circling the sun, and proclaimed the Scriptures are inerrant, hoping to prove Copernicus wrong. More on this later when we look at second-century Christian writings.

Next, we turn to Daniel and the importance of the oral law in carrying out obedience to God.

# 13

# Daniel and the Oral Law

## NO SATAN OR HELL

DANIEL, SHOULD NOT BE seen as part of the apocalyptic Jewish writings. It was written in 167 to 164 BCE, as part of the Ketubim (or Ketuvim) or "Writings" which were written to encourage the Hebrew people to maintain their faith that God will act. It is the only book of that period to be included in the Hebrew canon. Daniel is presented as a figure from the 585 BCE Babylonian exile. However, Pophyry, a Neoplatonic philosopher (ca. 234 to 305 CE), quoted in Jerome's *Commentary on Daniel*, recognized the period of Daniel's writing is after the reign of Antiochus IV Epiphanes, since Daniel 11:45 mentions Antiochus' death in 164 BCE. Thus, biblical scholars affirm that all of Daniel's so-called predictions are after the fact.

Daniel begins with a series of seven folk tales, each of which illustrates how civil disobedience against the oppressor is rewarded by Yahweh. The tales are designed to stiffen the Jews to hold fast, to remain faithful to the Jewish God, for in the end their own God is far superior to any other kings or gods. The tales cover the Hebrew prophets traditional promise for a day of liberation from oppressors and the promise that God would act.

The seventh tale is presented as Daniel's own vision. It is a vision of animals representing the progression of four kings that had controlled Israel from 586 BCE down to Daniel's time of 167 BCE. The winged lion is Babylon, the bear is the Medes, the four-winged leopard is the Persians, the dragon-like beast is the Greeks, and a little horn represents Antiochus IV Epiphanes through whose persecution they were suffering.

It is in this seventh vision or dream where there is a continued shift in the view of history. The prior hope was for a Davidic type human leader to rise up and bring a victorious new kingdom of shalom. But that mythic vision was no longer working. The writer of Daniel looks beyond human history for a liberator. He, too, recognized systemic evil as beyond human correction. Therefore, he looks to "one like a human being, coming with clouds of heaven" to whom will be given kingship over all people, nations and languages and who will serve him forever (Dan 7:13–14). Here the "one like a human being" represents the whole community of faithful Jews. Daniel fleshes out this vision. "The kingship and dominion and the greatness of the kingdoms under the whole heaven shall be given to the people of the holy ones of the Most High; their kingdom shall be an everlasting kingdom, and all dominions shall serve and obey them" (Dan 7:27).

We note this calls for an ideal divine kingdom as a center of humanity that other nations will serve and obey. The unspoken danger is Israel will strive to become the superpower of the nations with all the aggrandizement and self-rationalization that goes with supreme power and embrace the claim that Israel is doing Yahweh's will. Such rationalization has been the failure of all dominating systems.

In Daniel's closing chapters the writer recognizes that the Israelites have brought this calamity upon themselves; not through some outside satanic being or a fallen Watcher (Dan 9:8, 11). There is a desperate communal prayer for Yahweh's mercy for only in Yahweh's act will there be a new moral order. "We do not present our supplication before you on the ground of our righteousness, but on the ground of your great mercy. O Lord, hear; O Lord, forgive: O Lord, listen and act and do not delay! For your own sake, O my God, because your city and your people bear your name" (Dan 9:18–19).

In chapter 10:1, 13, 20, there is a mythic heavenly conflict between Michael, the patron angel of the Jews, and the patron princes of Persia and Greece. This heavenly conflict is thought to mirror the earthly conflicts during this period of history. In the end, Michael indicates there would still be a time of great anguish, but the people would be delivered and a new moral order would be established. In chapter 12:2 there is the allusion to a resurrection: "Many of those who sleep in the dust of the earth shall awake, some to everlasting life, and some to shame and everlasting contempt." This allusion speaks to the resurrection of the whole nation of Israel whose dry bones will come alive as projected by Ezekiel.

Even in the midst of conflict and chaos, Daniel maintains the monotheism of God and the concept of corporate sin of the nation, not the judgment of individuals. Evil is still the freewill choice of human beings of which all are guilty. There is no catastrophic destruction of everyone and everything on earth. The writer's vision centers on an end time for a new human community, a new moral order, that continues to be played out within human history and upon this earth. There is no Satan or hell in Daniel. Daniel is the only work of this period seen as reflecting acceptable Jewish thought and thus included in the Hebrew canon.

## THE ORAL LAW

The final picture we saw in the book of Jubilees was that the renewal of Israel and the whole creation will come through the study of and obedience to the laws of the Torah. It is this obedience that would bring the "End of Days" with the end of systemic evil as a Satan, a renewed garden of Eden, and the renewal of the covenant with Yahweh. "And the jubilees shall pass by, until Israel is cleansed from all guilt of fornication, and uncleanness, and pollution, and sin, and error, and dwells with confidence in all the land, and there shall be no more a Satan or any evil one, and the land shall be clean from that time for evermore" (Jub 50:5).

Because obedience to the law was so crucial for Jubilees we need to appreciate the development of the oral law. To begin, it is essential to understand the nature of Judaism as a revealed religion. According to this understanding, revelations were given to the mythic Adam, to Abraham, and especially through Moses for once and for all time. What a person is to believe and trust was what Yahweh had revealed, including the laws of the Torah. The revealed Torah was seen as the true revelation of Yahweh.

It was during this 596 to 536 BCE exile that the "Holiness Code" of Leviticus was developed to help explicate in more detail the laws of the Torah. The writer believed all their tragedy was happening because they continued to break the commandments of Yahweh. If so, then possibly a greater enforcement and expansion of the Torah law would prevent another disaster. Therefore, following the destruction of Jerusalem in 167 BCE, there began to be added what was called the oral law that was developed over a long period of time to meet the everyday circumstances of Jewish living. These laws were eventually codified between 165 to 200 CE into what is called the *Mishnah*. However, these new practical laws had to be consistent with the written Torah law for both claimed divine origin, divine authority, and were binding upon all Jews.

The ultimate purpose of the oral law was to place a "fence around the law" so no one could easily break it (Mish., *Aboth* 1:1). It became increasingly restrictive and reflected the culture of Judaism from about 200 BCE onward, including during Jesus' life. For the Sabbath alone there were listed thirty-nine prohibited acts as an attempt to define an "act of work" on the Sabbath. Over time, some of the strict Sabbath prohibitions were: sowing, ploughing, reaping, binding sheaves, threshing, winnowing, kneading, baking, weaving, making two loops, weaving two threads, separating two threads, sewing two stitches, tearing in order to sew two stitches, writing two letters, erasing in order to write two letters, putting out a fire, lighting a fire, taking anything from one house to another, etc. Even the distance one could travel on a Sabbath was restricted (Mish., *Shabbath* 7:2).

One of the important issues for this historical period was this tightening of the law which was seen as a means of preventing another exile and enabling the Messiah to come. It further tightened definitions of legality and illegality under which Jews would be separated into righteous or wicked camps. It also gave tighter definitions of Jewishness that again made sharper separations between the Jews and pagan nations. In Jubilees, obedience to the impersonal and unbending law became the measure of faithfulness, not the personal relationship of love and trust with Yahweh that we saw in the Sinai covenant. These differences will become very important when we examine Jesus and Paul.

We move in the next chapter to examine several key sectarian groups that developed after the Antiochus-Maccabean wars, namely, the Dead Sea Qumran community, the Pharisees, the Sadducees, the Essenes, and the peasantry to see their understandings of evil and punishment.

# 14

# Jewish Sectarian Groupings

WE NOW TURN TO the sectarian communities and parties that developed after the Antiochus-Maccabeans wars and which continued to exist throughout most of the first Christian century. Our time frame is 160 BCE to 70 CE. We will first look at the theology of evil, Satan, and hell in the Qumran sect that began about 140 BCE, existed during Jesus' lifetime, and continued up until about 70 CE. Second, we will look at the individual descriptions and theology of the Pharisees, the Sadducees, and the Essenes that also developed during this period. Third, we need to understand what was happening to the peasantry.

## THE THEOLOGY OF THE QUMRAN COMMUNITY

I am deeply indebted to Lawrence Schiffman and his work in *Reclaiming the Dead Sea Scrolls* for much of the following material that I will closely follow. Early scholars with the discovery of the Dead Sea Scroll concluded the Qumran community was composed of Essenes. However, later Jewish scholars such as Schiffman are convinced it was a small group of disaffected Sadducean priests. The Qumran community included families of women and children, which the Essene community forbade. The Essenes were a celebate community which only males could enter.[1] Schiffman feels these Sadducean priests bitterly objected to the chaos and corruption in Jerusa-

---

1. Schiffman, *Reclaiming the Dead Sea Scrolls*, 8–80.

lem concerning both the high priesthood and the temple, especially with installing a non-Zadokite as high priest in 152 BCE. Given this, they left the city after the Maccabean wars (168–164 BCE) to seek a new, more obedient life in the desert near Qumran located on the northwestern shore of the Dead Sea around 153 BCE.

A major task of the community was not only to be a holy community of the righteous, but also to collect sacred Jewish documents and to copy and preserve them from destruction during and following Antiochus IV Epiphanes' persecution. At one point during the persecution, all Torah scrolls were to be burned and those hiding them were to be executed. As a result of the discovery of these Qumran texts in 1967, we now have information about a largely unknown period of history from Alexander the Great (325 BCE) to the great Hebrew teacher Hillel (10 CE).

Schiffman is clear that these early Sadducean priests felt they were especially chosen by God to maintain the purity of the law and keep faith with their religious past. They saw themselves as forming a holy community that would be obedient to God in all respects. To them there were two parts to the law. First, was the revealed written law of the Torah. Second, was the hidden or secret law, known only to the sect and to be taught by the priests to others. Later, a Teacher of Righteousness is identified as a central leader of the group. This teacher was plagued by a "Wicked Priest" who represented the corrupt Hasmonean leaders back in Jerusalem.

The Qumran sect explained the existence of evil by moving to an extreme ethical dualism. We saw that Isaiah believed God was the author of both good and evil (Isa 45:7). The sect also believed this. But they believed neither good nor evil attributes could derive directly from God. So they developed an idea that God had created two spirits at the time of creation. There was a good spirit of light, truth, and righteousness. There was an evil spirit named Belial relating to the Belair we saw in Jubilees, who was a spirit of darkness and evil, and who opposed God.[2]

In Qumran thought, both spirits act as God's agents in the management of the world since each spirit has a group of human followers. One's entire life pattern of behavior was determined by to which group one belonged. These spirits were predestined to have dominion at different times. There were times of brutality and times of war; there were times of peace and times of harmony. At some points in the literature it appears that the two mythical spirits represent an internal struggle of an individual soul. At

---

2. Ibid., 149.

other points it appears the two spirits are external powers that compete for dominion over the entire cosmos. On earth there was a Teacher of Righteousness with his forces. Also on earth there was a Wicked Priest with his forces that were called the Kittim. The Kittim included not only the traditional enemy nations, but also fellow Jews who did not follow the Qumran community's interpretation of the Torah. The powerful elite in Jerusalem were viewed as heretical and must be destroyed.

Since these two forces were on earth, they felt there were two opposing forces in heaven. Michael was the name for the heavenly forces of Light. Belial was the name for the heavenly forces of evil. At the end of the age, there would be a great battle between these heavenly and earthly forces. The men of the Qumran community were thought to be fighting beside the good cosmic forces. After the final battle they would conduct a messianic banquet of bread and wine as described in the *Rule of the Congregation* for the religiously elect. The surviving faithful would reconstitute the life of Israel on its land in accordance with sect's views.

Only in the future age, after the war, would it be possible to completely observe the Torah as interpreted by the sect. Then the people of Israel would live a life of purity, even surpassing their current level of observing Jewish law. Their lives were dedicated to preparing for the new age by living as if it had already come. The *Rule of the Congregation* sets out the vision for the future community of perfect holiness that they were convinced would happen in their lifetime. There would be two messiahs. The priestly messiah Aaron would rule over a rebuilt temple and a lay messiah would rule as a political king.[3]

According to Schiffman, what is unique is that all has been predestined. Human beings have no real choice over the way their affairs will play out, either in individual terms or in national and cosmic senses. The divine plan is known only to God, not to humans.[4] This appears to be a major departure from the Jerusalem Sadducees, who, also according to Schiffman, felt human beings had absolute freedom of will and that God did not retain total control over them.[5] In the end the ultimate triumph of the good is assured since Yahweh is creator of both the good and evil powers and manages control over both. Michael and Belial are always subordinate

---

3. Ibid., 322–23.
4. Ibid., 147–48.
5. Ibid., 76.

Eliminating Satan and Hell

to Yahweh for the Qumran Jews never allowed an infringement upon the monotheism of Yahweh.

We must flag several Qumran convictions as we look ahead to the Christian era. First, that the community alone knew the will of Yahweh. This makes for a vast separation between the Qumran community as the just and the rest of the world as unjust and doomed to destruction in a final battle. Second, they pick up Belial from Jubilees as their name for systemic evil that would engage Yahweh in a final cosmic and earthly battle. Third, in this battle all humans who opposed the sect would be killed which seemed to justify the community's need for vengeance against the Jews in Jerusalem and the heathen nations. But it would make Yahweh a warrior god complicit in using violence that does not fit the compassionate Yahweh we have seen in the Hebrew canon. Fourth, one of their two Messiahs would be a kingly ruler, a role that Jesus rejected. Finally, in the Qumran community, we see not only an ethical dualism on earth of good and evil between the Wicked Priest and the Teacher of Righteousness, but also a cosmological dualism with two heavenly spirits fighting each other. However there is no blame for evil from an original sin of Adam and Eve or from the Watchers of Genesis as in 1 Enoch.

The community existed from about 150 BCE until about 70 CE when they were destroyed by the Romans as part of the campaign to crush the Great Revolt of the Jews against Rome (66–73 CE). Thus, their views were current during Jesus' life and up to the writing of Mark's gospel. A second major source of information on the parties within Qumran community is the historical *Works of Flavius Josephus*. So in looking at the theology of the Jerusalem parties of this period we will be using both Josephus and Schiffmann.

## THE SADDUCEES

The Sadducees were known from about 150 BCE. However, there are no known Sadducean texts and most of what is known comes from hostile sources. Since the Sadducees were opposite of the Pharisees, the rabbinical literature almost always portrayed the Sadducees as enemies. Sadducees were either priests or they intermarried with the high-priest families connected to the temple. They represented the nobility, the power and wealth of Israel. Being political realists, they tended to cooperate more closely with their Greek and Roman rulers, thus protecting more of their own power.

Even though their culture may have been greatly influenced by the Greek and Roman environment in which they lived, they maintained strict obedience to the written law of the Torah given to Moses.

They had serious differences with the oral law of the scribes and Pharisees for its inconsistencies. The Sadducees believed the Torah laws of purity applied only to the temple and the priest, and rejected the development of oral laws to make them apply to the total everyday life of the all Jews. They did not believe in the immortality of the soul and thus rejected any doctrines of the resurrection. Therefore, God's punishment must fall on the human community in this life not in some later hell. Continuing the theology of the prophets, they felt the judgment of Yahweh was upon the whole Jewish community and thus saw the exile as their punishment in the past and their subjugation by the Greek as their punishment in the present. They rejected the Pharisees' belief of fate governing all things. Since they did not believe Yahweh exercised control over human affairs, all human actions are the cause of what is good or evil. The people receive what is evil only as a result of their own foolish choices.[6]

From this we see that the Sadducees were not part of the stream of Jewish leadership through which apocalyptic ideas of a Satan and hell were transmitted. With the destruction of the temple in 70 CE, the Sadducees as a group and their temple duties ceased to exist.

## THE PHARISEES

Our second group is the Pharisees who represented primarily the middle and lower classes of Judaism that did not become Hellenized. The word for Pharisees (*perushim*) means to be separate. This possibly referred to their self-imposed separation from the *am ha'aretz*, "the people of the land," who were not learned in the law and who were careless about the laws of Levitical purity.

The Pharisees accepted as authoritative not only the ancient Torah traditions of Israel, but also what they termed as the "traditions of the Fathers." These were the unwritten nonbiblical laws and customs passed down through generations to meet everyday situations while at the same time not be in conflict with the written laws of Moses in the Torah. The scribes, backed by the Pharisees, would study the law and come up with a way to carry out a needed practical action. Eventually 613 very minute

---

6. Josephus, *Antiquities*, bk. 13, ch. 5, sect. 9.

and restrictive oral laws were developed over a long period of time to put a fence around the Mosaic law. This was a way of keeping people far from breaking the basic law and would secure God's good favor and save the people from further foreign oppressors (Mish., *Aboth* 1:1). The Pharisees embraced this oral law as being from Yahweh and of equal authority with the written Torah, thus they were extremely scrupulous in observing all of them.

The whole issue of justice and the law became very important to the Pharisees in defining who were the righteous and who were the sinners. As we have seen, when a code of laws becomes the measure of human activity, it can also become a legalistic god. The relationship is then one of measuring action to legalistic obedience to the law, rather than a relationship of love and trust to Yahweh. The law can only show a justice of legality or illegality and judgment, not mercy. It was at this point of legalism that Paul broke with the law and Jesus opposed the Pharisees.

> The Pharisees also held to a doctrine of rewards and eternal punishment.
>
> They believe the souls have an immortal vigor in them, and that under the earth there will be rewards or punishment, according as they have lived virtuously or viciously in this life: and the latter are to be detained in an everlasting prison, but the former shall have power to revive and live again.[7]
>
> They say that all souls are incorruptible; but that the souls of good men are only removed into other bodies—but that the souls of bad men are subject to eternal punishment.[8]

In this we hear overtones of Plato and 1 Enoch with immortal souls, an underground imprisonment and eternal punishment for the wicked, and reincarnation for the just. Thus, they had a concept of hell. Their belief, however, did not involve cosmological beings that cause evil since Yahweh had foreordained human actions and was therefore responsible for both good and evil. Thus, they had no belief in Satan. The Pharisees developed the synagogues to teach the masses their beliefs and were concerned that the spiritual life of the people should be centered in the synagogues. During Jesus' life, the Pharisees were a significant group with whom he was often in opposition. Following the destruction of Jerusalem in 70 CE, the Pharisees

---

7. Ibid., 13.1.3.
8. Josephus, *War*, 2.8.14.

became the most powerful group left and the only one with whom the Romans could work.

## THE ESSENES

The Essenes appear to be a branch of the Pharisees that literally abandoned Jerusalem. In protest against the way the temple was being run, they went out into the desert to prepare the way of the Lord. They believed all history is determined by Yahweh's hands governing everything. They practiced community in property and shared wealth equally. They did not marry wives, but lived by themselves and ministered one to another. Women were not allowed in their cult. Only adult males could enter the sect. In their initiation they "bound themselves by oath to be pious toward Yahweh, just to men, honest with their fellow Essenes, and to properly transmit the Essene teachings to other men."[9] As mentioned above, since the Qumran community was composed of both men and women, this is the reason Schiffman holds that it was not established by the Essenes. However, the Essenes also virtually ceased to exist after 70 CE.

## THE PEASANTRY

The peasantry is our final group, who were the people of the land, unsophisticated, largely illiterate, and untrained in the law. Nevertheless, they carried within their memories Yahweh's deliverance from Egypt under Moses and the powerful message of the biblical prophets that one day Yahweh would liberate Israel from all foreign occupation and a peaceable kingdom would be restored on earth. However, University of Massachusetts professor Richard Horsley reminds us that the governing classes of traditional societies almost always look upon the peasants as less than fully human.[10] It was the peasantry who always took the burden of domination by the Hebrew ruling elite. It was the peasantry who had to produce enough food for them to live on and enough extra to support the goods and tithes demanded by the high priesthood of the temple. It was also the peasantry who took the brunt of foreign occupations. First, it was the Assyrian occupation in 732 BCE, then the Babylonian conquest in 586 BCE, the Persians in 536 BCE,

---

9. Schiffman, *Reclaiming the Dead Sea Scrolls*, 79.
10. Horsley, *Bandits, Prophets, and Messiahs*, xxix.

the Greeks in 325 BCE, the Romans in 60 BCE, with all the subsequent brutality and slaughter. When foreign powers placed heavy levies on Israel, it was the peasantry who paid heavily in one form or another.

It was also the peasantry who desperately looked for a liberator, a messiah, to free the nation and restore harmony. The hope was always there for Yahweh to liberate them. It was out of the peasantry that messianic leaders and pseudo-kings arose to lead revolts, only to be crushed. They, too, looked for a day of judgment where the good would be rewarded and the evil punished.

It is not clear how greatly the hopes and beliefs of these common, illiterate peasants were shaped by the historical theology of the prophets, and how much by the years of occupying foreign powers with apocalyptic theologies of Satan and hell, rewards and punishment. There are no writings from this group and the Israelite leadership looked down upon them. As we have seen, they were called the *am-ha-aretz*, the people of the land, who could not read or know all the intricate laws or commandments of God. Thus, this whole segment of Israel was seen as beyond God's redemption. But it was among the peasantry that Jesus grew up, lived, and among whom he began his ministry. We will examine the plight and role of the peasantry more closely when we look at the period between 6 BCE and 135 CE.

## PRE-CHRISTIAN ERA CONCLUSIONS

As we close our look at the pre-Christian era it is significant to note that humanity has long struggled with the question of evil and its source.

We have seen the attempts of ancient Babylonian, Egyptian, Greek myths to project a supernatural explanation using mythic gods battling each other for supremacy among characters such a Marduk, Enlil, and Angra Mainyu. We have seen the Babylonian explanations of creation and humanity being born out of violent death in the *Enuma Elish* myth, resulting in a humanity of revenge and violence. Opposed to this was the Hebrew myth of Genesis 1, where out of the goodness of Yahweh all was created and all was "good" or "perfect."

Further, we have seen the Hebrew concept of hassatan (Satan) as one of Yahweh's creation, subordinate and always part of Yahweh's team. It was only later in the apocalyptic literature that this mythic hassatan began to change into a satanic opponent of Yahweh with differing names, Azazel, Belial, Mastemah, Prince of Darkness, each symbolizing a system of evil that was overpowering. We also saw the Hebrew Sheol as an underground place where everyone goes in a neutral death and no punishment. Later, in the Greek Septuagint, Sheol was wrongly translated as hades, which led readers to a concept of judgment and the possibility of eternal punishment. The location of gehenna in the Hebrew canon was clearly an above-ground valley.

But it was in the Greek and apocalyptic literature where we saw concepts of Tartarus and hades as vast storehouses of the dead deep in the earth, a concept which would no longer be sustainable by contemporary earth scientists. However, as Schiffman reminds us, this apocalyptic literature, such as in 1 Enoch and Jubilees, was never seen to contain the authorized record of God's revelation to humanity and was never included in the Hebrew canon.

We have seen concepts of justice being developed upon codes of law such as the Code of Hammurabi, the Torah and the oral law, rather than upon a covenantal relationship such as we saw in the Sinai covenant. This makes a shift of obedience from loving Yahweh, to obeying an impersonal law that can show no mercy, only judgment and punishment.

## POLITICAL AND THEOLOGICAL TRAJECTORIES

We have also seen several political and theological trajectories in Hebrew history. The first political trajectory is a shift from a dictatorial and ruthless rule such as in the *Enuma Elish* myth and the pharaohs, to a concept of Yahweh as a compassionate and reconciling Lord and King with co-commitments to the Jewish people. Threads of this Hebrew trajectory go all the way through the prophets, as seen in our chapters 6 and 7, where Yahweh's compassion and faithfulness is never diminished. When tragedy struck during the 586 BCE Babylonian captivity there were those who held firmly onto the trust that Yahweh would bring about a new heaven and a new earth based on the faithfulness of Yahweh's commitment to Israel in the Sinai covenant.

A second political trajectory developed when the Hebrews established a kingdom under Saul and David. This was always problematic as human kingships undercut the kingship of God. During and following the 586 BCE Babylon exile, Ezekiel's vision was that the dry bones of Israel would be rejoined and a new kingdom under God as Shepherd would be established. A new temple would be completed as Yahweh's home, ushering in a peaceful kingdom through the temple elite. However, in this new kingdom the people would still be subject to the ruling priestly elite with their interpretation of the Torah law and the developing oral law. When this kingdom did not arrive and the people were still suffering, there were others who began to seriously question where was Yahweh's justice?

The third trajectory, which I would label as theological, was seen in Jewish apocalyptic writings such as in 1 Enoch, Jubilees, and in the Qumran community. These concepts were mythic answers to the failed expectations, the continued oppression, and inter-Jewish conflict during the Greek occupation. This trajectory developed the separation of the righteous and the unrighteous based upon strict legality. This expectation borrowed from Plato that justice demands a reward of glory for the just and punishment for the unjust. In this apocalyptic trajectory we saw the Hebrew concepts of hassatan and Sheol being changed. We began to see a variety of names for systemic evil, Azazel, Belial, Mastemah, that was opposed to Yahweh, and a distinct location of a place of punishment. This trajectory, however, was never accepted as an authoritative revelation of Yahweh by the Jews. Furthermore, according to the gospels there is no indication that Jesus ever quoted from the apocalyptic literature. The only New Testament quote from this literature is from 1 Enoch in Jude 1:6.

The fourth trajectory, which I would call both theological and political, was developed in the servant passages of Second Isaiah. There we saw Yahweh's promised restoration of Israel to be based on a return to the Sinai covenant relationships with Israel being copartners with Yahweh to enlighten, teach, and heal the world of nations. The role of Israel was to be a servant, not a dominating power over other nations. The concepts of Satan as an enemy of God and hell as a place of eternal punishment are not part of this trajectory. We will see major elements of this trajectory picked up in the life and quotes of Jesus and the gospels.

Finally, in the basic Hebrew canon, Yahweh is a God of justice, but more importantly a God of compassion and restoration, of reconciling people and all of nations. This is not an angry, punitive god who punishes all nations and/or individuals whom Israel would identify as enemies. Nor is Yahweh a god who will annihilate all humanity and destroy everything else to blot out sin and start all over again. As we approach the Christian era we need to watch carefully how these trajectories, if any, play out.

Again, I would stress that myth, as I have been using it, is not fairy tale stuff, but an attempt to explain life for the people who lived in a time of very limited knowledge. They knew the reality of systems of evil and gave personalized names to them. However, the names were mythic and figures of speech for evil, not real historic entities. I find no basis in the Hebrew canon upon which to develop a concept of an angry, evil god named Satan, nor of a place of eternal punishment named hell.

# 15

# First-Century Political Conflict

WHEN WE TURN TO the first Christian century we find a continued hardship and conflict that is essential for us to understand. The basic realities of the *Enuma Elish* myth were still very much alive that humans were created to serve the powerful. The Romans under the despised Herod still occupied Palestine. The co-commitments with God of the Sinai covenant had again been compromised or forgotten. It was during this period that Jesus was born and to which he ministered.

The political setting we find is that Palestine had become an essential part of the Roman empire when it was conquered in 63 BCE. Since the grain of Egypt sustained Rome's populations, Rome could not afford to lose control of this vital land route down the eastern side of the Mediterranean Sea for economic and military reasons. However the Jews would never willingly submit to Roman occupation any more than they did to Greek occupation.

Jacob Neusner, Jewish research professor of religion and theology at Bart College, comments, "Rome scrupulously would do everything possible to please Jewry, permitting the Jews to keep their laws in exchange only for peaceful acquiescence to Roman rule. There was, alas, nothing Rome could actually do to please Jewry except vacate Palestine. No amiable tolerance of local custom could suffice to win the people's submission."[1]

---

1. Neusner, *First-Century Judaism*, 43.

## HEROD: 40 TO 4 BCE

In 42 BCE the Hasmonean Jewish ruler, Antigonus, tried to retake control of Judah. However, he was crushed when Herod occupied the whole of Galilee and laid siege against Jerusalem in the spring of 37 BCE. None of the Jewish defenders, including Antigonus, were spared. There are differing evaluations of Herod. Scholars such as Richard Horsley show a cruel picture of harsh punishment for anyone who opposed him.

> The punishments given to those caught were harsh, and both openly and secretly many were brought to the fortress Hyrcania and executed. Both in the city and on the open roads there were men who spied on those who met together. . . . Those who obstinately refused to adapt to such social constraints he punished in all kinds of ways . . . and those who showed some spirit and were indignant at his forcing [the loyalty oath] he got rid of in any way possible.[2]

It is clear that Herod eliminated opposition from the old Jewish leadership and developed a new power base among the high priests and nobility that were loyal to him. But it was also clear that the peasantry carried the heaviest burdens. They were the ones who had a hard enough time making a living, who had to pay high rents to the landowners, and were taxed from one-fourth to one-third of their annual production. It is no wonder that many of these common people were seething with resentment. They were the marginalized ones at the lowest economic level and many of the so-called bandits who came from this group began waging protests. This was the cultural climate and countryside within which Jesus was born in 4 BCE. In his ministry he was speaking to hard-pressed, overtaxed, often hungry peasants who were struggling for their livelihood. Were they not the very people whom Yahweh claimed as his people and who had promised to protect them?

At Herod's death in 4 BCE, the Jerusalem populace, reinforced by Passover pilgrims, mounted a sustained protest and revolts erupted in the countryside. Athronges, a common shepherd from the Judean hills along with his brothers, led villagers in a successful guerrilla war that effectively regained Jewish independence from Rome for three years. However, in retaliation the Roman general Varus burned many towns and devastated the countryside. He scoured the hills for rebels and eventually had about two

---

2. Horsley, *Bandits, Prophets, and Messiahs*, 33.

# Eliminating Satan and Hell

thousand men crucified. He also enslaved some thirty thousand people in and around Tarichaeae on the Sea of Galilee. Sepphoris, near Nazareth, and Emmaus were destroyed.

Apart from Josephus, from 6 to 26 CE there are no direct records of this period that would be helpful to scholars. Thus, we pick up history again with Pontius Pilate's rule in 26 to 36 CE. Early in his reign Roman standards with images of Caesar on them were brought into Jerusalem. This was against Jewish sacred law and the Jews begged for them to be removed. Pilate refused, declaring he would kill them if they did not accept the standards. Then, "as if by arrangement, the Jews all fell down to the ground, extended their necks, and proclaimed they were ready to be killed rather than transgress the law. Astonished by the intensity of their religious fervor, Pilate ordered the immediate removal of the standards from Jerusalem."[3]

A second revolt occurred when Pilate took Jewish funds from the temple treasury to pay for the building of an aqueduct to bring water into Jerusalem. Again, thousands of Jews protested. Only this time Pilate did not relent. Josephus writes: "Since he had foreseen the disturbance, Pilate had planted a troop of soldiers among the crowd, disguised in civilian clothes. They had orders not to use swords, but to beat any hecklers with clubs. He then gave the agreed signal from his tribunal. Many Jews were killed."[4]

We must recognize the status by which the Roman population held their emperors, namely as gods. When Octavian took on the new name of Augustus, he was acclaimed as a "god and the Savior of the world" and was seen as divine. Thus, when messianic pretenders gathered followers to challenge the authority of their Roman rulers they were brutally killed.

## THE RISE OF THE BANDITS

Over the next forty years there were many "bandit" protests led especially by the Essenes. They were those who championed the historic values of justice and raged against injustice. These bandits could see themselves as protectors of the poor, as the defenders of traditional religious values and representing divine justice. Thus the bandits and brigands were usually protected by the peasantry who saw them as championing justice and freedom. Some bandit leaders arose claiming to be new Davidic kings. Others

---

3. Josephus, *Antiq.*, bk. 18, ch. 3, sec. 1.
4. Josephus, *Wars*, bk. 2, ch. 9, sec. 4.

claimed to be the long hoped-for messiah. Each gained a following of supporters and each Pilate suppressed with immediate violence.

By the middle 40s to 50s CE, even the scribal scholar-teachers, called the Sicarii, began to fight back with kidnappings and assassinations against the priestly aristocracy who, in order to retain their power, had collaborated with the Romans. The priestly elite were soon seen as the true enemy of Judaism. During the summer of 66 CE, another severe famine occurred and a widespread revolt erupted in Jerusalem and throughout the countryside. The people of Jerusalem attacked the leading high priests and their mansions in an armed revolt. Again, the Romans put it down by slaughtering many and sought a divide and conquer strategy. As the banditry increased dramatically in the countryside, the Romans moved into Judea in the fall of 67 CE, devastated the countryside, its villages, and inhabitants. The peasants had no alternative but to flee from their homes or to join the brigand groups.

## JOHN OF GISCHALA

One of the small villages the dreaded Romans approached was Gischala, which wanted peace. However, a man in village, named John, favored war and encouraged the villagers to rebel. While the Roman general Titus surrounded the town, John of Gischala tricked him not to attack on the Sabbath. On that day John fled the city with his armed men and escaped to Jerusalem. When he arrived in Jerusalem he found it had no governor. So he took over and tried to persuade the people of the city to go to war against the Romans. The aristocracy and leading people of the city opposed this and forced John and his men to take refuge in the temple and its fortress. Nevertheless, John's group retained enough control to elect a high priest who was considered to be unworthy of the office.[5] Soon John became so tyrannical that the aristocracy and general population could no longer tolerate his bandits and sought a means to overthrow him.

## SIMON OF GIORA

The aristocracy then turned to another man named Simon, son of Giora. He also had gathered his own gang of bandits and had ravaged many parts

---

5. Josephus, *Wars*, bk. 4, ch. 3, sec. 8.

of the countryside. However he was promising "liberty to those in slavery, and a reward to those already free, and got together a set of wicked men from all quarters . . . so that his army was no longer composed of slaves and robbers, but a great many of the populace were obedient to him as their king."[6] When Simon of Giora and his band arrived outside the walls of Jerusalem, John of Gischala and his bandits were inside ready to fight against them. The innocent population of Jerusalem now faced being caught in a deadly battle between two sets of Jewish bandits.

## THE BATTLE FOR JERUSALEM

Jerusalem's old high priests then assembled the people and asked them what should be done to avoid the assault. Josephus describes the result:

> In order to overthrow John (of Gischala), they determined to admit Simon, and earnestly to desire the introduction of a second tyrant into the city: which resolution they brought to perfection, and sent Matthias, the high priest, to beseech this Simon to come into them, of whom they had so often been afraid. . . . The people also made joyful acclamations to him, as their savior and preserver; but when he was come in with his army, he took care to secure his own authority, and looked upon those that invited him to be no less his enemies than those against whom the invitation was intended.[7]

Now the city was caught in a major civil war between three groups: John's gang of bandits, Simon's gang of bandits, and the city aristocracy. At this point the trapped innocents called for the Romans to rescue them. The Roman general, Titus, came in the spring of 70 CE to help and the siege of Jerusalem began. By summer the walls were breached and by September the Romans were in total control. The historian Neusner writes: "Many were killed and many more sold into slavery until Jewish captives glutted the slave markets and arenas of the Empire. The Temple was burned."[8] John of Gischala was imprisoned. Simon of Giora surrendered in such a way as to reveal that he thought of himself as the messiah, so the Romans executed him as the "king of the Jews." Once again Israel was completely under the dreaded control of Roman occupation.

---

6. Ibid., ch. 9, secs. 3–4.
7. Ibid., sec. 11.
8. Neusner, *First-Century Judaism*, 154.

# First-Century Political Conflict

By this time the whole political and religious alignment had drastically changed. The Sadducees had lost all popular support. The Essenes had lost all respect. The Zealots had been the staunchest of anti-Roman warriors but had now been beaten down. Neusner describes the situation. "All that now was left was the workaday world. Politics had ended. The Temple lay in ruins. The piety lavished at the altar flowed wastefully to the ground. Jews ruled little more than their own home and hearth. The 'house of Israel' now consisted of villages and towns, no longer of a state."[9]

## WHY HAD THIS TRAGEDY HAPPENED?

The ultimate question for the Jews remained: Why? The people had to be told why they had to endure such suffering. Neusner gives a long, painful word-picture of their agony, parts of which I will extract because I feel that most of us have never realized what a painful period this was for the Jews. The Romans saw it one way: "To [the Roman Centurion] and his cohorts the Jews seemed never to be satisfied, no matter how carefully the government respected their rights and sensibilities. . . . 'What do these Jews want?' the centurion must have wondered, and what keeps them in ceaseless turmoil?"[10] The Jews saw it another way:

> This land is holy, given by God, who made heaven and earth, to the people of Israel, whose sons and offspring we are. It can be governed properly only by those to whom God has given it, not by pagans.[11] All Jews affirmed the holiness of Jerusalem the faithful city. . . . They were sure that by learning what Jeremiah, Ezekiel, and (Second) Isaiah taught about the meaning of the catastrophe of 586 B.C., by keeping the faith which prophecy demanded, they had ensured the city's eternity. . . .[12] "It is a holy city, and its work is the service of God on high." The temple was the center of the world. To it in time would come the anointed of God.[13]
>
> What had the Lord commanded of old, which now they did not do? As to ancient Scriptures, were these not studied in the synagogues Sabbath upon Sabbath. . . .[14] The priests were always

9. Ibid., 173.
10. Ibid., 18.
11. Ibid., 19.
12. Ibid., 20–21.
13. Ibid., 23.
14. Ibid., 22.

careful to keep the levitical rules of purity which God decreed, they thought, just for this place and hour. . . . It was not a *sinning* generation, but one deeply faithful to the covenant and to the Scriptures that set forth its terms.[15] . . . That war was waged not for the glory of a king. . . . It was a war fought explicitly for the sake and in the name of God.[16]

Neither wisdom, wonder-working, nor sacrifice saved Jerusalem. When it was destroyed, some men lost the will to live. . . . Some regarded the destruction as the final day in Israel's history and expected the last judgment to take place then. With the Holy of Holies and the city and the temple in flames, they awaited the conclusion of history.[17]

Since they lost, later generations looked for their sin, for none could believe that the omnipotent God would permit his temple to be destroyed for no reason. As after 586 B.C., so after 70, the alternatives were this: "Either our fathers greatly sinned, or God is not just." The choice thus represented no choice at all. "God is just, but we have sinned—we, but mostly our fathers before us. Therefore, all that has come upon us—the famine, the exile, the slavery to pagans—these are just recompense for our own deeds."[18]

Neusner's painful description indicates the Jews did not turn to Jewish apocalyptic explanations for their defeat. They had no Azazal or Belial opposing God and the people, nor punishment in a fiery hell for all those who were destroying everything dear to their historic heritage and beliefs. The people were responsible for the calamity by their own deeds. However, it was during this terrible period of history that Jesus lived, ministered, and was killed. It was when Paul wrote his letters to the Gentiles, and Mark, Matthew, Luke, and John wrote their gospels. It was not a pretty century.

After this bitter defeat in 70 CE there are also two major Jewish writings, 2 Baruch and 2 Esdras, which give insight on serious questions being asked. Both books continue to wrestle with the issue of evil and the theodicy question we have been looking at since the beginning of this project. Both books are listed in the Pseudepigrapha.

15. Ibid., 25.
16. Ibid., 26.
17. Ibid., 132.
18. Ibid., 26.

## 2 BARUCH

Second Baruch contains a profound theological dialogue between Baruch and God. Why had God let this happen? If there is nothing better in life than the persecution they are undergoing, nothing could be more bitter especially if there is no justice at the end. There is a search for the cause of such evil, and we find in 2 Baruch that though Adam sinned he is not the cause.

> For though Adam first sinned And brought untimely death upon all, Yet of those who were born from him, each one of them has prepared for his own soul torment to come, And again each one of them has chosen for himself glories to come. . . . Adam is therefore not the cause, save only of his own soul. But each of us has been the Adam of his own soul.[19]

We see a continuation of the doctrine that death came into being when Adam sinned. But it was because the Jews, who by their own choice had failed God and now must suffer the consequences of those choices. Baruch uses *Sheol* in the traditional sense as "those who sleep in the earth."[20] There will be a resurrection when the souls of the righteous will be made like angels; the wicked will know torment and their souls will simply waste away.[21] But there is no eternal place of fire and punishment, no Tartarus, or hades, and no Satan in Baruch. There is no cosmic battle between God and evil forces as in the Qumran writings. The evil was caused by the people's own choices.

God tells Baruch they have not been abandoned but were being disciplined for their own good. At the end time the earth will be renewed, no one will die untimely, women will no longer have pain at childbirth, and God will restore Israel. In 2 Baruch, God is concerned and gracious: "He will continually remember you, He who always promised on our behalf to those who were more excellent than we, that He will never forget or forsake us, but with much mercy will gather together again those who were dispersed."[22]

Second Baruch, though being written during extremely depressing times, continues the basic historical Hebrew understanding of Sheol and

---

19. 2 Baruch 54:15, 19.
20. 2 Baruch 21:24.
21. 2 Baruch 51:5–6.
22. 2 Baruch 78:6–7.

the conviction of a compassionate God who will restore Israel. Second Baruch does not buy into any of the apocalyptic myths we have seen in our chapter 12.

## 2 ESDRAS

The second writing is 2 Esdras, the main body of which (chapters 3–14) was written twenty to thirty years after Jerusalem's destruction. The author takes the name of Ezra, and he, too, wants to know why his people had to suffer so greatly. This time the dialogue is between Ezra and Uriel, one of God's spokespersons whom we also met in 1 Enoch. There is a vivid picture painted of Jerusalem's horror. Ezra bitterly complains that Israel's sins were no worse than other nations, especially Babylon's. Why punish Israel and not them? Ezra insists mortals must be able to comprehend something of God's ways. If not, life has no purpose at all.

In 2 Esdras there is an interesting shift from 2 Baruch in that God has little compassion for sinners.

> Let many perish who are now living, rather than that the law of God which is set before them be disregarded! For God strictly commanded those who came into the world, when they came, what they should do to live, and what they should observe to avoid punishment. Nevertheless they were not obedient, and spoke against him; they devised for themselves vain thoughts, and proposed to themselves wicked frauds; they even declared that the Most High does not exist, and they ignored his ways.[23] . . . I will not grieve over the great number of those who perish, for it is they who are now like a mist, and are similar to a flame and smoke—they are set on fire and burn hotly, and are extinguished.[24]

The Jews have made their choices, let them suffer the results. However, there is a concept that the "disease" of sin began with Adam. "For the first Adam, burdened with an evil heart, transgressed and was overcome, as were also all who were descended from him. Thus the disease became permanent; the law was in the people's heart along with the evil root, but what was good departed, and the evil remained."[25] "O Adam, what have you done? For though it was you who sinned, the fall was not yours alone,

---

23. 2 Esdras 7:19–25.
24. 2 Esdras 7:60–61.
25. 2 Esdras 3:20–22.

but ours also who are your descendants."[26] The writer is clear that although Adam sinned, he is not alone the cause of the current evil which brought such catastrophe. Thus there is no blaming of either God or any sub-gods such as a Satan.

In 2 Esdras the disease of systemic evil is certainly thought of as an enemy of God, but it is not personalized with a name. There is a judgment of sinners, but it is not clear if they are simply destroyed, wander about in torment forever, or burn in the pit of fire. All three concepts are there. As a book of despair, questioning, warning, and hope for the Jews at this tragic moment of their history, 2 Esdras' message was: "Take courage, O Israel; and do not be sorrowful, O house of Jacob; for the Most High has you in remembrance, and the Mighty One has not forgotten you in your struggle."[27]

## THE BAR KOKHBA REVOLT, 135 CE

But for the Jews, the destruction of Jerusalem in 70 CE was not the end of tragedy. Hadrian, who was the Roman emperor, saw them as continuing troublemakers. His actions did not help when he began building a new temple to Jupiter on the sight of the Jewish temple. He also prohibited Torah law, and established Jerusalem as a Roman city in hopes Judaism would cease to be. To the Jews this meant either the death of their faith, or for Jewish guerrilla forces to renew their attacks on the Romans occupiers. This time under the banner of Simeon Bar Kochba, a Jewish messianic movement was formed and fought overwhelmingly against the Romans. For three years Judea was basically independent. But in 135 CE, the Romans brought in massive forces and once again the rebellious Jews, who wanted nothing more than freedom on their own land, were "annihilated, exterminated, and eradicated from the land."[28]

There was no longer a homeland the Jews could call their own, and would not be until 1948 CE. There remained only pockets of dispersed Jews in the villages and cities of foreign nations such as in Alexandria. Had God forgotten his chosen people? Had God finally damned them for not being loyal according to the ancient commandments and the law? This Hebrew sociopolitical climate of the first and second Christian centuries was far more oppressive and brutal than Christian writings reveal.

26. 2 Esdras 7:48.
27. 2 Esdras 12:46–47.
28. Horsley, *Bandits, Prophets, and Messiahs*, 129.

## Eliminating Satan and Hell

One of the purposes of looking at these first-century Jewish history and writings is to see where, after the painful tragedy of Jerusalem's destruction, the Jews would locate the source of evil. Both of these, 2 Baruch and 2 Esdras, kept it squarely on human choice, not on a Satan, or Mastemah, or Beliar. This is a consistent Jewish answer from the Genesis 2–3 myth, through the prophets, and now through this tragedy. The monotheism of Yahweh has remained uncompromised and there is no sub-god named Satan, and Sheol has retained its neutral historic Jewish meaning.

In the next chapter we begin looking at Christian literature of this same period, starting with the letters of Paul.

# 16

# Paul on Satan, Sin, Hell, and Related Concepts

IF THE FIRST CHRISTIAN century Jewish writings did not buy into the apocalyptic trajectory, what did the earliest Christian writings do? Paul is our earliest source for the beliefs of the early Christian community. It is he who wrote letters to young Gentile churches before the tragedy of Jerusalem's destruction and before any of the four gospels were written. Systemic evil was very much alive within Judaism as well as from the Roman occupation. I will be looking at how the terms "Satan" and "hell" were used by Paul and at his view of the Creator-God. In doing so I will focus only on Paul's seven undisputed letters and his basic theology.[1]

---

1. Scholars have struggled with what are authentic Pauline writings—which are his, which are questionable, and which are definitely not. Seven Pauline letters are generally classified as "undisputed":
- 1 Thessalonains, ca. 51–52, the earliest of all New Testament writings
- Galatians, ca. 56–57, written very close to his Romans
- Corinthian Letters, ca. 53–56
- Philippians, ca. 56–57
- Philemon, ca. 55–56, written most likely when Paul was in Ephesus
- Romans, ca. 57–58, but probably 58

Six additional letters bearing Paul's name do not currently enjoy the same academic consensus: Ephesians, Colossians, 2 Thessalonains, 1 & 2 Timothy, and Titus. Of these six, the first three have no consensus on whether they are or are not authentic Pauline letters. First and 2 Timothy and Titus are widely regarded as pseudepigraphic, though some conservative scholars consider them genuine.

## Eliminating Satan and Hell

As we approach Satan in Paul, and later in the gospels, the excellent work of my doctoral professor visiting at the Hartford Seminary, Walter Wink, is a helpful place to begin.

> It is only in the period between the Testaments, and even more in the period of the New Testament and early church, that Satan gains recognition. Soon he will become known as the Enemy of God, the Father of Lies, the Black One, the Arch-Fiend, and assume the stature of a virtual rival to God. We will come to all that. But first, we must do justice to those passages in the New Testament where Satan continues to function as a servant of God. So accustomed are most of us to thinking of Satan as purely evil that we tend to read this interpretation into passages where there is nothing of the kind. If we suspend that bias, the evidence points toward a strikingly different picture.[2]

One of the challenges in working with this historical period is the temptation to ascribe to Paul our contemporary concept of Satan as a personalized enemy of God sitting in some far-off celestial abode gleefully manipulating humanity to do evil, and to see hell as a repository of endless fire and pain for the punishment of sinners. This is what Wink warns against. The ancients used these mythic symbols as their way of defining their world. Continuing their symbols for our present world can be terribly misleading. Wink asks if there is any way we can re-symbolize evil?[3] Wink's question is very important. As I have been pointing out, the mythic symbols of Satan and hell do not fit what we now know about our world. My response to Wink is to dismantle the symbol of Satan and to use the term "systemic evil" which is more of what the Satan term symbolizes. Then we are better able to comprehend the reality of evil and own it.

For example, we can understand systemic greed and evil in what Bethany McLean and Joe Nocera describe in *All the Devils Are Here: The Hidden History of the Financial Crisis*. In their 2010 book, Debbie Killian, a mortgage broker, is quoted: "It is clear to me that a slow creep took over . . . a slow moving slime that ultimately permeated the industry. I have this picture of lava . . . just creeping along until every business was covered with it, eventually getting smothered."[4] We can understand this kind of evil. We can understand the systemic evil of Nazism and Communism in Alan

---

2. Wink, *Unmasking the Powers*, 14.
3. Ibid., 11.
4. McLean and Nocera, *All the Devils*, 213.

## Paul on Satan, Sin, Hell, and Related Concepts

Wolfe's book *Political Evil: What It Is and How to Combat It*. These kinds of "systemic evil" are realities we can own . . . we can do something about them. We cannot do this with a mythic Satan in the far-off reaches of the universe doing evil on the earth. Therefore, in the following chapters I will try to use the term "systemic evil" where appropriate instead of Satan.

As we examine Paul we need to separate: (a) where "Satan" functions in a similar way to the Hebrew hassatan . . . as God's faithful attorney general, (b) where Satan functions as a figure of speech representing a human system of evil that is opposed to God, and (c) where, if ever, Paul used the term "Satan" for a personalized cosmological god as found in apocalyptic literature.

## IN 1 THESSALONIANS

In 1 Thessalonians, Paul's earliest letter, Satan is used only once. Paul had a fruitful first visit with the budding Christian community in Thessalonica, but now longed to see them again. We do not know what kept him away. Whatever it was, Paul used the symbol of Satan as what blocked his early return. "For we wanted to come to you—certainly I, Paul, wanted to again and again—but Satan blocked our way" (2:18). Here we see that Paul used Satan in a similar manner to the Hebrew hassatan, as a hinderance to his desire to visit, and not as the cosmic enemy of God.

## IN 1 CORINTHIANS

In 1 Corinthians, Satan is used twice. The first use is 5:45. The context is about the man in the Corinthian congregation who was sleeping with his father's wife. Evidently the congregation was willing to tolerate this. Paul's concern was that tolerating such behavior opened the congregation to tolerating even more unacceptable Christian behavior. Paul says the man "should be handed over to Satan for the destruction of his flesh." The language sounds severe, but verse 2 and 13 indicate this only meant excommunication from the congregation, as Wink points out. "Satan is to work him over through the choice forced upon him by the act of ceremonial exclusion (and possible shunning), that 'his spirit might be saved'—at least on Christ's return, but possibly, through Satan's good offices, rather immediately."[5]

---

5. Wink, *Unmasking the Powers*, 15.

Handing the man over to "Satan," i.e., excommunication, served God's purpose as a restorative act, not a destructive one.

Paul appears to be speaking about the same man in 2 Corinthians 2:5–11. If so, the man did repent and Paul asked the congregation to forgive him and reaffirm their love for him. Again, Paul used the symbol of Satan similar to the Hebrew hassatan, one of God's agents to heal the man so as not only to restore him to the unity of the congregation but also to restore the ethical integrity of the congregation itself. If the church had self-righteously refused to forgive the repentant man, that would be playing the same role of hassatan in Zechariah 3 as the accuser, where God had already forgiven him.

Again, as Wink points out: "Satan's role here is remarkably fluid. Satan is again God's holy sifter.... And most astonishing of all, Paul does not say that Satan enticed this man to sin; rather, Satan is the means of his deliverance. This understanding of Satan has little in common with the remarkably evil Satan of popular Christian thought."[6]

The second use in 1 Corinthians is found in 7:5 where Paul encouraged a husband and wife to have a normal sexual life rather than abstinence. Here he used the Satan term as a tempter for whatever false attitudes the couple had which kept them from having a healthy sexual life. Such abnormal sexual restraint would "tempt" them to go outside the relationship for sex due to "lack of self-control." The interesting point in this episode is that sexuality is not the root of evil but encouraged between husband and wife. The symbolic "Satan" is acting as the Hebrew hassatan, i.e., for their good, not their destruction.

## IN 2 CORINTHIANS

In the composite letter of 2 Corinthians, the Satan term appears twice. In the first use Paul was concerned that egotism and boasting on his part would be wrong (12:7). He saw the thorn in the flesh as a message from Satan to make sure he was boasting about what God was doing not about what Paul was doing. Again, the symbolic Satan was acting as the Hebrew hassatan, a corrective influence, not evil.

The second usage is found in 11:13–15, where super-apostle "boasters" were giving false teaching about Christ. Paul warns his followers not to be taken in by these people; even Satan can appear as "an angel of light" and

---

6. Ibid., 16.

thus be deceiving. Paul recognized there are many voices in the context of living that, while appearing to be good, tempt people the wrong direction. Here, we see "Satan" not so much as a cosmic person, but as that possibility in every human choice: one that moves us closer to following the will of God, or one that serves self and follows inner voices which take us away from faithful servanthood. The inner and outer voices one listens to most can become either a god or a Satan. It was about this that Paul was warning his followers not to become dupes or agents of systemic evil. In each of these passages, Paul is using Satan as the Hebrew hassatan, as an agent bringing about something good.

However, in 2 Corinthians 6:14–15, Paul clearly uses a different term: *Beliar*. "Do not be mismatched with unbelievers. For what partnership is there between righteousness and lawlessness? Or what fellowship is there between light and darkness? What agreement does Christ have with Beliar? Or what does a believer share with an unbeliever? What agreement has the temple of God with idols? For we are the temple of the living God; as God said."

We saw this *Beliar* term (which means "worthless") in Jubilees and the Qumran War scrolls. Beliar is the symbolic name for that which embodies destructive elements of lawlessness and darkness that pull against God and deny God. In the Qumran War Scrolls, Beliar is very much an opponent of God and is used as a symbolic contrast between righteousness and lawlessness. Here, Paul is saying that Christ would have nothing to do with this kind of mythic Belair, and urged the Corinthians to follow Christ, not be followers of evil systems surrounding them in their culture. Here Paul is quoting a Qumran designation.

## IN ROMANS

In Romans there is only one use of Satan and that is in the final farewells. "The God of peace will shortly crush Satan under your feet. The grace of our Lord Jesus Christ be with you" (16:20). There has been much commentary on whether chapters 15–16 are Pauline or later additions by the early church. There is a general consensus by scholars that 16:20 is not authentic Pauline, but a scribal interpolation. Therefore, it is inappropriate to attribute this passage as Paul's thoughts on a Satan.

What we see in Paul is that he used the Satan term primarily as the Hebrew hassatan, the obstructer, the tempter with false teachings. But we also saw Paul reaching for something deeper. He understood that God had, from the beginning, given humans the freedom to make choices. Within the countless social, economic, personal and institutional powers beckoning for attention, there are temptations for everyone to become captive to systemic evil that is satanic. Paul recognized this dimension of struggle within all humanity. Being tempted and captured by wrong choices gives power to evil; and humans become coconspirators with it.

## PAUL'S UNDERSTANDING OF SIN AND EVIL

Paul has a complex understanding of sin. In Romans, Paul turns back to the Genesis 2–3 myth of the fall. It is clear to him that systemic evil is not a recent thing but extended as far back as humans had been on earth and involved in power systems that were self-serving rather than God-serving. In the Genesis 2–3 myth, we saw that the terms "Adam" and "Eve" were symbolic terms for generic "humanity" and "life," not the first man and first woman. Paul reaches back and uses Adam as a symbolic part of this historic humanity where sin first began. "Therefore, just as sin came into the world through one man [i.e., humanity], and death came through sin, and so death spread to all because all have sinned" (Rom 5:12). This does not imply an "original sin" that is sexually and genetically inherited from Adam down to all subsequent generation. But it does recognize that systemic evil was part of the powers and structures which humans created down through history.

The important point Paul was making is that from the beginning of human history, the Jewish and Gentile communities have been surrounded and controlled by governing authorities and institutions that were systemically evil. Paul understands these authorities and institutions as originally created by God and were needed by societies to function harmoniously. "Let every person be subject to the governing authorities; for there is no authority except from God, and those authorities that exist have been instituted by God" (Rom 13:1). But when these systems ceased to serve God's purposes and instead turned to serve purposes that are destructive and dehumanizing, they then became systemically evil. It is also clear that the authorities, powers, and institutions that surrounded Paul's culture had gone amuck. Both Jewish and Gentile communities stood in need of breaking free from this bondage, this "sin," which he saw as bringing death to the human spirit and destruction to God's kingdom in the human community.

For Paul, then, Christ's death and resurrection is a defeat of this systemic evil. A compassionate God in Christ opened the door to reconciliation, moving humanity into a reconciled oneness with God and each other, which is the meaning of and goal of the kingdom of God. This kingdom was not for the end of history, nor only as a heavenly entity for the righteous after death, but for all people on earth and for Paul's time. He writes:

> For the love of Christ urges us on, because we are convinced that one has died for all; therefore all have died. And he died for all, so that those who live might live no longer for themselves, but for him who died and was raised for them.
>
> From now on, therefore, we regard no one from a human point of view; even though we once knew Christ from a human point of view, we know him no longer in that way. So if anyone is in Christ, there is a new creation: everything old has passed away; see, everything has become new! All this is from God, who reconciled us to himself through Christ, and has given us the ministry of reconciliation; that is, in Christ God was reconciling the world to himself, not counting their trespasses against them, and entrusting the message of reconciliation to us. So we are ambassadors for Christ, since God is making his appeal through us; we entreat you on behalf of Christ, be reconciled to God. For our sake he made him to be sin who knew no sin, so that in him we might become the righteousness of God. (2 Cor 5:14–21)

In Paul's understanding of evil, he was not dealing with the cosmic Satan of contemporary religious fantasy. He was dealing with the deep inner choices and constructs of humans surrounded by all the authorities and institutions of systemic evil that were denying God.

## WRATH AND PUNISHMENT

In Romans 1:18, Paul stated: "For the wrath of God is revealed from heaven against all ungodliness and wickedness of those who by their wickedness suppress the truth." Then immediately in 1:24, 1:26, and 1:28, Paul stated three times that "God gave them up" to the freedom of pursuing their lust, their passions, their debased minds as they choose. Wrath or punishment is simply God handing human beings over to the consequences of their own deeds. Here I turn to the insights of two contemporary scholars on this important concept of wrath. First, to Ernest Käsemann's *Commentary on Romans*:

Eliminating Satan and Hell

> The concept of the wrath of God, which is common in Paul, does not derive from Greek tradition, but from O.T. Jewish apocalyptic. Hence it is not to be viewed as an emotion nor set within the framework of a moral world view. . . .[7]
>
> He [God] exercises judgment by delivering up the guilty to the separation from God which they want. Their wish becomes their fate and therefore the power which rules them. Conversely this power lets them once again become what they wish and do, namely creatures in the corruption of creatureliness.[8]

Käsemann does not see wrath as an inner emotion of God, but a God who "gives up" humans and nations to do what they wish even while God knows that destructive historical events will eventually catch up with them. Paul's use of "wrath" then is the cause and effect chain of historical existence where human beings are punished by the very evil they choose and commit. The punishment is within this life.

Supporting Käsemann are further comments of Stephen Travis, New Testament scholar at St. John's College, Notingham, England, in *Christ and the Judgement of God*, who begins his chapter on the wrath of God: "The question to be asked here is: does wrath involve the idea of retributive punishment, or is it perhaps a way of saying that God allows people's wrong choices to reap their consequences, to arrive at an inevitable conclusion?"[9]

Travis continues this concept where wrath for Paul was primarily a broken relationship with God and God hands people over to the inevitability of their own actions. His conclusion parallels Käsemann's. Wrath for Paul, then, was not the image of sinners in the hands of an angry God, but of a God who, in giving humans the freedom of choice, sorrowfully hands them over to the painful results of wrong choices.

## PAUL ON HELL

Given this understanding of God's actions, Paul stayed clear of Plato's and the Jewish apocalyptic concepts of hell that we saw in earlier chapters. Bernstein comments:

> Paul did not have a clear idea of hell. His concern was more intently focused on the positive side of the Christian message. He

---

7. Käsemann, *Commentary on Romans*, 37.
8. Ibid., 43–44.
9. Travis, *Christ and the Judgement*, 54.

## Paul on Satan, Sin, Hell, and Related Concepts

never used the word "Gehenna," and in the one place where he refers to hades it is in the context of celebrating the resurrection of the flesh, the defeat of death. "Death [*thanatos*] is swallowed up in victory." "O death [*thanate*], where is thy victory? O death [*Hade*] where is thy sting?" (1 Corinthians 15.54–55).... It is sufficient to note that the point of Paul's only reference to Hades is to celebrate its impotence![10]

In this 1 Corinthians 15 passage, Paul is combing two Old Testament passages that scoff at death. Isaiah 25:7 reads: "He [the Lord] will swallow up death forever. Then the Lord God will wipe away all tears." Hosea 13:14 reads: "O Death where are your plagues? O Sheol, where is your destruction?" In Paul's Septuagint translation of Hosea it would have read "hades" instead of Sheol as we have noted before. Thus, it is safe here to assert that Paul was speaking of the Hebrew Sheol, not Plato's eternal punishing hell. Travis makes two other important points affirming this conclusion:

> There is no allusion to disciplinary punishment of unbelievers (though l have found rare hints of this in the Apocrypha and Pseudepigrapha). But it is noticeable that Paul generally refuses to allow any clear-cut anticipation of the final judgement in its aspect of condemnation.[11]
>
> People's destinies, therefore, will be a confirmation and intensification of the relationship with God or alienation from him which has been their experience in this life. Retribution, however, is really incompatible with this sphere of ideas. For retributive punishment involves dealing with an evil by inflicting a fresh evil—which is exactly the opposite of the idea that God leaves humanity to experience the inherent consequences of their self-chosen alienation from him. Similarly, in Paul's view, eschatological salvation is the continuation and consummation of a relationship with God already experienced. To call this "reward" in the strictly retributive sense would be like calling marriage a reward for being engaged. Judgement, then, means for Paul not so much that retribution is imposed on people's deeds, as that, "Those who have lived in fellowship with God continue in that relationship, and those who have turned their backs on him continue in that outer darkness they have made for themselves."[12]

---

10. Bernstein, *Formation of Hell*, 207.
11. Travis, *Christ and the Judgement*, 209.
12. Ibid., 211.

Paul believed those who believed in Christ will inherit the kingdom of God; those who do not believe will not (1 Cor 6:9). The consequences of human choice and punishment is played out in this life. Therefore, he mentioned no place of hell for those not in Christ except that they will not know the glory of God's Kingdom on earth.

## FAILURE OF THE LAW

Paul saw the law as one of the road blocks to reconciliation. We examined in our chapter 13 how restrictive and suffocating both the written and oral law had become. It was obedience to this legal system that defined Jewishness and gave the Jewish hierarchy its power base to justify or condemn a person or a nation as evil and against God. Gentile nations, who never had the law, were seen as apostate. The poor Jewish "people of the land," the peasants who had never learned all the laws, were seen as beyond salvation. There could be no reconciliation with such unbelievers. Paul was rejecting this. In the Galatians letter, some Jewish Christians were insistent on retaining their Jewish law and its circumcision requirements along side their new Christian beliefs. Paul's answer to them was "no."

Paul justified his answer on the basis that God had blessed Abraham four hundred years before the law ever existed (Gal 3:17). What defines faithfulness, therefore, is not obedience to the law, but the nature of the covenant relationship established between Yahweh and Abraham. If that faith relationship encompassed the love, trust, obedience and service as seen between Jesus and God, then God openly welcomes them (Gal 2:16).

Finally, in Romans 8, Paul sees God's reconciling actions until "the creation itself will be set free from its bondage to decay and will obtain the freedom of the glory of the children of God" (Rom 8:21). Humanity does not stand alone in futility. For Paul the workings of the Spirit were bringing about a transformation from evil's destructiveness to a "freedom of glory" which will extend beyond humans to the whole of creation. This new creation will not be complete, however, until all earthly economic, political and social systems are committed to the will of God. When this kingdom is complete, then Christ will hand it over to God.

## CONCLUSION

This can be safely stated in two brief sentences. First, Paul's focus was on Christ's actions of healing and reconciling the brokenness of the human community, not on an apocalyptic Satan or hell. Second, for Paul, God's end goal is a new creation, not condemnation and destruction.

# 17

# Satan in the Gospels

As we explore Jesus' use of Satan in this chapter, we need to keep in mind that we are working within two crucial frameworks. First, Jesus was an historical Jew, born and educated within the Jewish culture. As a student of the Hebrew canon, he would have known the Hebrew understanding of hassatan as an adversary for God, not as an enemy. He would also have known the Hebrew Sheol as a neutral, non-punishing place of death. Second, we have already seen Yahweh in the Hebrew canon as compassionate, forgiving, reconciling and never breaking the divine side of the covenant relationship with Israel. It was the theology of Paul that in Jesus, "the fullness of God was pleased to dwell" (Col 1:19), and in John, "No one has seen God. It is God the only Son . . . who has made him known" (John 1:18). Therefore, if Jesus is revealing the nature of God and inaugurating a new kingdom of God, then he must be, as New Testament professor Herman Waetjen asserts, "The one who is so completely and perfectly human that the image of God will become transparent in his life and activity."[1] With these two frameworks in mind, we begin our examination of Jesus' use of the Satan term.

---

1. Waetjen, *Reordering of Power*, 72.

## THE BAPTISM

The gospels begin with the baptismal scene. Mark 1:9–11 is copied in Matthew 3:13–17 and Luke 3–21–22. In each of these gospels it was the Spirit's voice that defined Jesus' future ministry with two roles: (a) the Servant passage of Second Isaiah 42:1, and (b) the Messianic coronation passage of Psalm 2. The term "Messiah," which historically stood for one who would exercise God's character and authority on earth, is now combined with a Servant role. This is a radical departure from apocalyptic concepts of Azazel, Belial, Mastemah, or Satan as cosmic gods who punish with eternal pain. This departure is important to recognize. For we will find that Jesus' use of such terms as Satan and hell relate with, and give transparency to the compassionate, loving image of God we have been seeing throughout the Hebrew canon.

As God's Servant Messiah on earth, Jesus must confront how he will carry out his Servant commission given the culture in which he was living. . . . Up to now he had been surrounded by a cultural situation defined by Walter Wink as "the spirit of an entire society alienated from God, the great system of mutual support in evil, the spirit of persistent self-deification blown large, the image of unredeemed humanity's collective life."[2]

In his simple baptism Jesus rejects this corrupt human system and departs from it. After a full immersion in the Jordan's waters, he rises to let flow away all obligations to the evil power systems, the corrupt religio-political structures, the wrong laws and regulations that had surrounded him. He rises from the waters taking on an obligation of complete trust and commitment to God. The old "Adam" had failed. Jesus became the new "Adam," the New Human Being, commissioned to create a radically different kind of human community. This baptism was a powerful symbol of who he was as the Servant Messiah and what he was to confront.

## THE TEMPTATION SCENE

This leads us into the temptation scenes. In Mark, the scene is brief: "And the Spirit immediately drove him out into the wilderness. He was in the wilderness forty days, tempted by Satan; and he was with the wild beasts; and the angels waited on him" (1:12–13). In Matthew and Luke, a detailed threefold scene is copied from "Q." However, in each gospel's passage it is

---

2. Wink, *Unmasking the Powers*, 24.

## Eliminating Satan and Hell

the Spirit of God, not an evil being, that initiated Jesus' act of going into the desert. This was his time for a deep internal searching about what his future role would entail. For centuries, the Jewish community had looked forward to a new David-like kingdom, freed from the oppression of foreign powers, freed from frequent famines, freed from crippling diseases and death. Were these not the expected promises of God in the voices of the Prophets? Wink spells out this powerful temptation to follow what was expected:

> What is Satan tempting him with here and in each of these "temptations," if not *what every one knew to be the will of God?* Mosaic Prophet, Priestly Messiah, Davidic King—these were the images of redemption which everyone believed God had given them in Scripture. (And in no time at all they would be the titles given Jesus by the church: Prophet, Priest, and King.) What irony: everyone in Israel knew the will of God for redemption—except Jesus. He was straining with every nerve to hear what it was *as if he alone did not know it.*
>
> And Satan's function in all of this? He is no archfiend seducing Jesus with offers of love, wealth, and carnal pleasures. Satan's task is far more subtle. He presents Jesus with well-attested scriptural expectations which everyone assumed were God's chosen means of redeeming Israel. . . . Satan offers him, in short, not outright evils but the highest goods known to Israel.[3]

The power that tempted Jesus was not some cosmic god. Rather, it was the systemic evil of popular expectations, those invisible forces to maintain the religious and political systems of the old order. For a new kingdom of God to be birthed, the power of these popular expectations had to be rejected. Here, the gospels use Satan as the Hebrew hassatan (Job's tempter) and Jesus' struggle with and rejection of all the evil systems that controlled the Jewish people. These systems were structured to satisfy the Jewish elite and the power of Rome, but not God.

We must make a mental shift here. It is my conviction that we need to rename the term Satan and call it for what it is: "systemic evil." In our last chapter we saw Professor Wink had asked if there is any way we can re-symbolize evil? My response then was that we need to eliminate the term Satan. Jewish apocalyptic literature gave personal mythic names to concepts of evil to help them explain their world. But we do not live in that world and those mythic names no longer work to explain our world. If we fail to make this re-symbolization, our focus will always be on some cosmic

---

3. Ibid., 18.

untouchable evil god. By calling it systemic evil we will better understand the reality of the enemy against which Jesus was struggling, namely, the powerful forces of evil in his culture . . . a systemic evil that was being caused by humans and is alive at every historical level including our own. I recognize my representing Satan as systemic evil is a different understanding than found in most contemporary minds. But it is a switch we must make if we are to fully understand what Jesus was confronting, and what we must confront in our society. For every time Jesus spoke of a kingdom of God, he was confronting the political kingdom of Rome and the religious powers in Jerusalem. This was a daunting and dangerous undertaking!

Thus, in this temptation scene and throughout Jesus' ministry, it was the cultural systemic evil that surrounded him, which sorely tempted him, but which he rejected. Where the symbolic Adam, representing the old humanity, had failed, Jesus as the New Human Being was determined to remain true to God. With these evil power systems, Jesus will be in conflict until his death on the cross. With the victims of systemic evil, i.e., the poor, the peasants, the sick and the blind, the rejected and the outcasts, Jesus will have compassion throughout his ministry. Wherever the mythic Satan term is used in the gospels, either by Jesus or the writers, we will see the transparency of a compassionate, healing God in Jesus fighting against systemic evil.

## THE BEELZEBUL SCENE

In the Beelzebul scene of Mark 3:19b–30, copied in Matthew 12:22–37 and Luke 11:14–23, we find Jesus was reversing cultural expectations by healing the very outcasts who were not allowed into the temple. The scribes, feeling threatened, used this popular mythic symbol of Beelzebul to accuse Jesus of being in cahoots with the prince of demons. Jesus responded by refuting their logic and used their mythic "Beelzebul" term back against them. If he is in league with evil, how can he cast out evil? That would be working at cross-purposes.

Here the gospels use the term Satan as part of Jesus' response. "If Satan is divided against himself how will his kingdom stand?" Jesus was not setting up a cosmological Satan, but simply responded to the scribes and used their popular apocalyptic symbols back at them showing he was doing God's work, not the work of corporate cultural evil. In this exchange, Jesus brings a sharp criticism against his socio-political world. It is a judgment that cannot help but outrage the political and religious elite who benefited from the status quo. The usage of Satan in this passage is as a mythic representation for human systemic evil, not as a separate evil being in the cosmos.

### PARABLE OF THE SOWER SCENE

In this scene, original in Mark 4:1–20, copied in Matthew 13:36–43 and in Luke 8:4–18, the term Satan is used: "Satan immediately comes and takes away the word that is sown" (Mark 4:15). The passage is changed to "devil" in Matthew and Luke. Jesus, having told the parable to the disciples, finds they did not understand it. With some indignation, Jesus changed the parable from sowing seed to sowing the word. Jesus is using the language of rural Galilee in a way that counters popular apocalyptic expectations. Those expectations were for a cataclysmic in-breaking of God and a new creation in the near future. Jesus is proclaiming that the kingdom of God does not come at the end of a cosmic battle and Armageddon. Rather, the word of God, through him, is presently being sowed, being allowed to germinate, and will quietly grow to completion on earth. This is what Jesus was beginning to accomplish as he freed himself from obligations to the destructive structures and powers. This is also what Jesus was attempting to help his disciples understand. Here Satan is, again, not a cosmic personage, but the systemic forces of a culture which seeks to undo loyalties to God by distraction and pulling people away from God.

### PETER'S CONFESSION SCENE

In this scene of Mark 8:27–33, copied only in Mathew 16:13–33, Jesus asked the disciples who other people thought he might be. It was Peter who answered, "You are the Messiah." When Jesus said he will have to die, Peter strongly objected and took Jesus aside and began to rebuke him. But Jesus rebuked Peter and said, "Get behind me, Satan! For you are setting your mind not on divine things but on human things." Jesus was not calling his friend Satan. But he was calling Peter's expectation wrong and counter to the very essence and content of the new human community that was developing through Jesus' ministry. Jesus understood the oppositional fate that faced him from the evil power structures centered in the temple and in Roman rule. Peter and the disciples had not yet realized this.

In the temptations and the three scenes above, the Satan term occurs, but the term is used mythically and symbolically as a name for the systemic evil in human systems that challenged Jesus. Jesus is redefining old concepts of kingship and messiahship and reshaping them into new understandings of what loyalty means in the new kingdom of God . . . the New Human Community.

## THE RETURN FROM THE MISSION OF THE SEVENTY

Mark, Matthew, and Luke each mention a sending out of the twelve disciples, but only Luke in 10:18–20 has this scene of seventy returning. "The seventy returned with joy, saying, 'Lord, in your name even the demons submit to us!' He said to them, 'I watched Satan fall from heaven like a flash of lightning. See, I have given you authority to tread on snakes and scorpions, and over all the power of the enemy; and nothing will hurt you. Nevertheless, do not rejoice at this, that the spirits submit to you, but rejoice that your names are written in heaven.'"

Here in Luke 10:17, the demons submitted and the seventy come back rejoicing at their success. Jesus rejoices along with them saying, "I watched Satan fall from heaven like a flash of lightning." The quote has connections to Isaiah 14:15, where those who aspire to divinity fall to the nothingness of Sheol. Here the seventy represent the New Human Community bringing the powers of cultural evil into submission. Represented by the mythic term Satan, systemic evil will eventually fall and would no longer have dominion over the new human community that is beginning to grow.

## THE CRIPPLED WOMAN IS HEALED

In this story, found only in Luke 13:10–16, the debate between the leader of the synagogue and Jesus centers on the Sabbath law. The oral law, later embodied in the Mishnah, forbade such healing on the Sabbath unless a life was endangered (Mish., *Shabbath* 22:6 and *Yoma* 8:6). Jesus stressed that relieving the woman of her ailment on the Sabbath was as important as the Mishnah's allowing one to lead a donkey to water on the Sabbath. Jesus then ended with this question: "'And ought not this woman, a daughter of Abraham whom Satan bound for eighteen long years, be set free from this bondage on the sabbath day?' When he said this, all his opponents were put to shame; and the entire crowd was rejoicing at all the wonderful things that he was doing" (Luke 13:16–17).

The key point is Jesus' challenge of the law. First, that Jesus is not obligated to a Sabbath law that keeps humans from finding wholeness. And second, that God's reign is already working. Certainly our current medical community would not, nor would Jesus today, describe the woman's ailment being due to a Satan or a demon.

## JUDAS AT THE SUPPER

Mark, in 14:10–11, indicates that Judas had already decided to betray Jesus. Matthew follows Mark but indicates that Judas went first to the priests. Only Luke 14:10–11 and John 6:70, 13:02, and 13:27 have added the demonizing claims that Satan or the devil had entered into Judas. This passage raises questions. Was Satan one of God's mythic attorney generals, as in Job, testing Judas . . . a test he failed? If so what kind of God would be testing Judas on the issue of betraying God's own Son? This makes no sense.

I personally believe that Judas was a true believer who knew Jesus was the Messiah. And if pushed to the limit, Jesus would then act to bring in angels on a cloud and inaugurate the promised kingdom of God. This would fulfill the great Jewish expectations of a Messiah. But when that didn't happen and his Messiah was crucified, Judas, in remorse, hanged himself. Matthew seems to supports this.

Only in Luke and John do we find the Satan term related to Judas. Is this their editorializing a justification for Jesus death? We do not know. However both were written after the destruction of Jerusalem and during the time of separation between Judaism and Jesus' followers. What is clear is that Judas' betrayal fulfilled systemic evil's intent and power to destroy the new kingdom that Jesus was bringing into existence. It is crucial to see that it was not a cosmic Satan acting in Judas, but the human failure of Judas to understand Jesus' Suffering Servant ministry.

## PETER AT THE TRIAL

The Satan term again shows up in Luke 22:31–34: "'Simon, Simon, listen! Satan has demanded to sift all of you like wheat, but I have prayed for you that your own faith may not fail; and you, when once you have turned back, strengthen your brothers.' And he said to him, 'Lord, I am ready to go with you to prison and to death!' Jesus said, 'I tell you, Peter, the cock will not crow this day, until you have denied three times that you know me.'" In this passage Satan is in the role of the Hebrew hassatan, as one who sifts out the strength of Peter's belief. Here Jesus uses the Satan term as a sifter (not as an angry cosmic god), praying that Peter's faith won't fail, but knowing that Peter will eventually deny him.

In these passages from the Synoptic Gospels of Matthew, Mark, and Luke the Satan term appears as a mythic symbol for the human systemic evils found throughout Jesus' culture. Against this systemic evil, Jesus brings condemnation and judgment. As a power against Jesus, this systemic evil will resist his message and eventually nail him to the cross.

## THE DEVIL IN JOHN

We must recognize that in the gospels, but certainly in John, there were two time periods being addressed. The first is the time period of Jesus' life as the writers remembered what he said and confronted in his immediate situation. The second time period was thirty to seventy years later, when books were written to address situations then occurring. This was after the loss of the temple, after the end of the Sadducees and Essenes, and the rise of the Pharisees with their collaboration with Rome. Judaism was redefining itself, but also the Christian Community was separating itself from Judaism. This was especially true with John's gospel. As biblical scholars T. J. Wray and Gregory Mobley comment:

> Much of John's rhetoric against the Jews reflects the dire situation of his community in 90 to 100 CE. . . . For John, anyone who opposes Jesus' mission . . . is acting as a tool of Satan. . . . John does not depict Satan appearing as a freestanding supernatural being, rather, Satan appears in the guise of those people who oppose Jesus (and the Johannine community). . . . In his temptation episodes, John recasts the *people* in the role that Satan occupied in Matthew and Luke. In the latter, for example, Satan had tempted Jesus with political authority over all the kingdoms of the world (Mt 4:8-9; Lk 4:5-6). By contrast, in John it is the people who tempt Jesus, drafting him to be their king: "When Jesus realized that they were about to come and take him by force to make him king, he withdrew again to the mountain by himself" (Jn 6:15). The temptation to turn stones into bread (Mt 4:3; Lk 4:3) is transformed by John

> into an occasion when the people, rather than Satan, cite Scripture in an effort to coax Jesus into miraculously producing bread.[4]

It is important to recognize in this passage the shift by John of placing the role of a Satan onto the people who, in 90 to 100 CE Judaism, were also part of the systemic evil religio-political climate. It also important to recognize with Stephen Travis, lecturer in New Testament at St. John's College, Nottingham, England, that John is both "Jewish and anti-Jewish . . . both apocalyptic and non-apocalyptic. . . . Yet when we consider this gospel's treatment of divine judgement, the evidence is strikingly one-sided in that retributive elements are almost entirely absent."[5] In John, God is consistently transparent in Jesus as compassionate, not retributive.

## JOHN 6:61–70

In this passage Jesus tells the disciples that they must eat of his body and drink of his blood. This is a difficult passage for the faithful Jews and/or the disciples to understand and turned many people away. John adds:

> Because of this many of his disciples turned back and no longer went about with him. So Jesus asked the twelve, "Do you also wish to go away?" Simon Peter answered him, "Lord, to whom can we go? You have the words of eternal life. We have come to believe and know that you are the Holy One of God." Jesus answered them, "Did I not choose you, the twelve? Yet one of you is a devil." He was speaking of Judas son of Simon Iscariot, for he, though one of the twelve, was going to betray him. (John 6:67–70)

The passage reveals the reason why many of Jesus' Jewish followers and even some of his disciples would no longer follow him. Jesus was not fulfilling the popular expectations of a Messiah. He even asks the Twelve if any of them wanted to leave. Judas in this passage is simply named as a human betrayer who would desert Jesus.[6]

---

4. Wray and Mobley, *Birth of Satan*, 126–27.
5. Travis, *Christ and the Judgement*, 262.
6. For a thorough discussion of these conflicting expectations regarding Jesus, see Galambush, *Reluctant Parting*.

## JOHN 8:44

This passage continues the two-time-period issue: Jesus' lifetime and a time after the 70 CE destruction of Jerusalem. In both periods the Jewish community headed by the Pharisees thought they were the faithful community. A group of Jews were saying, "We have one father, God himself." Jesus counters, "If God were your father, you would love me. You are from your father the devil." Jesus counters that they are still stuck in their father's old world order that is systemically evil.

## JOHN 13:1-30

In this passage John sets up the betrayal scene by telling us, in 13:2, that the decision to betray Jesus had already entered into Judas before the Last Supper. The mythic devil here represents all those systemic evil forces that fought against Jesus and were determined to destroy him. In verse 27, Judas' decision was concretized by the end of the supper. Jesus knew it and told Judas to get on with the betrayal. Jesus fully recognized how a systemically evil culture had treated others with death who claimed to be the Messiah. Thus, Judas' betrayal and the cross were systemic evil's massive battle against Jesus and the attempt at stopping the growth of a new human community. Jesus was ready for it because he trusted his Father, and he knew the victory that was to be his in the resurrection. The "devil" terms are here, again, mythic uses of language in trying to explain why Judas did what he did.

## CONCLUSIONS

Hassatan in basic Hebrew thought was simply an adversary of Yahweh, testing and sifting human beings. This understanding had been used from the Adam and Eve myth, through the prophets, in Paul, and now in the gospels. It was human choice that caused evil, not some cosmological Satan as was seen in the divergent apocalyptic literature. What I find in the gospels is the Satan term being used as the traditional Hebrew "adversary" and also as a mythic representation for human systemic evil that opposes God and dehumanizes people. How we interpret these passages into today's understanding of our world and our human condition is significant. If we retain an anti-god Satan in a cosmic sphere as the human enemy yet to be destroyed, we then escape our accountability for evil, and allow chaos to continue undefeated until the end of time.

However, if we see in these passages where the new human community *has already begun* and has the power to defeat the anti-god earthly cultural forces of dominance and oppression, then we can own our responsibility for these anti-god forces and know that they can be defeated. As Q says, "The kingdom of God is within you!" (Q 17:21), or as the gospel of Thomas says, "The Father's kingdom is spread out upon the earth, and people don't see it" (113). Jesus is saying that the work of the kingdom in opposing systemic evil is here and now.

Given this, I am convinced that it is essential for us to drop the term Satan, which comes out of ancient myth and has been used for centuries as a cosmic anti-god personage wrecking havoc in humanity on earth. It is better to use the term of human systemic evil for that which infects and destroys human beings, institutions, and systems. Systemic evil is far more realistic for what is happening in our day. It is a far more understandable description of the human predicament than the apocalyptic and mythical names of Belial, Satan, Mastemah.

What we do see in the gospels is that Jesus embodies the very highest expectations of the prophets. It was back to the prophetic literature, not the apocalyptic, from which his quotations came, especially from Isaiah and Daniel. Therefore, we should realize Jesus' use of Satan is as a mythic symbol for the hassatan of the Hebrew canon, i.e., as one of God's agents to test and to bring about good. If we wish to identify evil in our society, it is far better to use the term systemic evil. We can wrestle with that. We cannot wrestle with a cosmic apocalyptic Satan that in reality does not exist. Next we turn to the term hell in the gospels.

# 18

# Hell in the Gospels

As we approach concepts of hell in the gospels we cannot forget Neusner's description of the painful political chaos before and after the fall of Jerusalem in 70 CE. During this time the whole political and religious alignment was changed drastically. Would a neutral Hebrew Sheol, with no concept of reward or punishment, still be a sufficient explanation to satisfy the hunger for justice to be paid by oppressive sinners if not in this life then in an afterlife? Remember, Paul had concentrated on the glories of the resurrection, but he never used the terms Sheol, hades, or Tartarus.

We also need to remember the terms that came from Greek literature and were introduced to the Jews during the Greek occupation. Hades in the Eleusinian Mysteries was where the unjust were judged by Persephone before being sent on down to Tartarus for punishment. In Plato, the incurably wicked were first cast into hades and then into Tartarus where they suffered everlastingly torment. Tartarus was located far below hades. We also saw levels of hell in the apocalyptic literature.

We remember the Hebrew term of Sheol was translated into hades in the Greek Septuagint. This changed the meaning of a neutral Sheol into hades that had been seen as a place toward punishment. These mythic terms of hades and Tartarus (and gehenna) are used in New Testament writings and get translated in our Bibles as hell. With these translation histories in mind, let us begin with gehenna in the gospels.

Eliminating Satan and Hell

## THE USE OF GEHENNA

In our chapter 11 we examined the Valley of the sons of Hinnom located outside Jerusalem into which the rebellious people who have done evil will be dumped. Yahweh, through the voice of Jeremiah, had proclaimed that all of Judah and Jerusalem would end up there if they did not change their dishonoring ways.

> And in this place I will make void the plains of Judah and Jerusalem, and will make them fall by the sword before their enemies, and by the hand of those who seek their life. I will give their dead bodies for food to the birds of the air and to the wild animals of the earth. And I will make this city a horror, a thing to be hissed at; everyone who passes by it will be horrified and will hiss because of all its disasters. (Jer 19:7–8)

This valley was clearly visible to all who passed by and is the one referred to in Isaiah 66:24: "And they shall go out and look at the dead bodies of the people who have rebelled against me; for their worm shall not die, their fire shall not be quenched, and they shall be an abhorrence to all flesh." Though the text of Isaiah 66 does not mention gehenna, as we saw in our chapter 11, the first-century Jewish Targum had: "will not die and their fire shall not be quenched, and the wicked shall be judged in Gehenna." Thus the Targum shows the development, after the Babylonian exile, of this visible Valley of Gehenna, as a shameful burial place for those who reject the ways of God. This gehenna is not a Greek hades nor Tartarus, nor our contemporary concept of hell. Yet the Greek term gehenna is Jesus' choice term for a place of punishment, since it appears eleven times in Matthew, Mark, and Luke, and Jesus uses it in five different settings.

## THE FIRST GEHENNA SETTING

The first setting is in Mark 9:43–48, where gehenna is used three times but only in this one incident where Jesus is quoted:

> If any of you put a stumbling-block before one of these little ones who believe in me, it would be better for you if a great millstone were hung around your neck and you were thrown into the sea. If your hand causes you to stumble, cut it off; it is better for you to enter life maimed than to have two hands and to go to *gehenna* [hell], to the unquenchable fire. And if your foot causes you to

stumble, cut it off; it is better for you to enter life lame than to have two feet and to be thrown into *gehenna* [hell]. And if your eye causes you to stumble, tear it out; it is better for you to enter the kingdom of God with one eye than to have two eyes and to be thrown into *gehenna* [hell] where their worm never dies, and the fire is never quenched.

In this passage, Mark quotes Jesus as passing judgment upon those who offend "little ones" because an offense against them was seen as an offense against God. There are three parallel indictments. The first is to be thrown into the sea. Obviously the sea is an above-ground location. The second and third indictments are be thrown into gehenna. According to Mark, Jesus concludes these indictments with "where their worm never dies, and the fire is never quenched." This, as noted above, is a quote from the Targum on Isaiah 66:24. In Mark, Jesus used the infamous Valley of Gehenna as an above ground location where those who offended God would be tossed after death. Therefore, Jesus' gehenna was not the underground hades or Tartarus of Plato or apocalyptic literature. In this passage Jesus' understanding of punishment takes place at death. This is not the hell of most contemporary teaching, where resurrection is followed by a sentence of eternal punishment.

Matthew takes the same setting from Mark and uses it in two different narratives. In his chapter 5 passages he use Isaiah's fire but not worm. In his chapter 18 passage he uses fire again.

> But I say to you that if you are angry with a brother or sister, you will be liable to judgment; and if you insult a brother or sister, you will be liable to the council; and if you say, "You fool," you will be liable to the *gehenna* [hell] of fire. (Matt 5:22) . . . If your right eye causes you to sin, tear it out and throw it away; it is better for you to lose one of your members than for your whole body to be thrown into *gehenna* [hell]. And if your right hand causes you to sin, cut it off and throw it away; it is better for you to lose one of your members than for your whole body to go into *gehenna* [hell]. (Matt 5:29–30) . . . And if your eye causes you to stumble, tear it out and throw it away; it is better for you to enter life with one eye than to have two eyes and to be thrown into the fire of *gehenna* [hell]. (Matt 18:9)

But in neither of these passages does Matthew change the basic meaning of gehenna from Mark's original passage. These Mark and Matthew settings are not repeated in Luke or John.

## THE SECOND GEHENNA SETTING

According to Q, Jesus states: "And do not be afraid of those who kill the body, but cannot kill the soul. But fear . . . the one who is able to destroy both the soul and body in *Gehenna*" (Q 12:4–5).

As indicated in our chapter 1, the Q document is an early source of Jesus' sayings that both Matthew and Luke have copied. In Matthew 10:28, this passage is: "Do not fear those who kill the body but cannot kill the soul; rather fear him who can destroy both soul and body in *gehenna*." In Luke 12:5, it is: "I tell you, my friends, do not fear those who kill the body, and after that can do nothing more. But I will warn you whom to fear: fear him who, after he has killed, has authority to cast into *gehenna*." Each implies the authorities can kill the body, but not the soul. Only God can destroy both. Again, note how gehenna is used. I find no reason to see its use as any different from Isaiah 66:24 or as in Mark. Namely, as the visible valley into which sinners are disgracefully tossed. It should be noted there is no illusion to a resurrection and then a punishment in these passages as was seen in the apocalyptic literature.

## THREE OTHER GEHENNA SETTINGS

The same question remains about gehenna in the other three passages where Matthew used the term. They are:

> You have heard that it was said to those of ancient times, "You shall not murder"; and "whoever murders shall be liable to judgment." But I say to you that if you are angry with a brother or sister, you will be liable to judgment; and if you insult a brother or sister, you will be liable to the council; and if you say, "You fool," you will be liable to the *gehenna* of fire. (Matt 5:21–22)
>
> Woe to you, scribes and Pharisees, hypocrites! For you cross sea and land to make a single convert, and you make the new convert twice as much a child of *gehenna* as yourselves. (Matt 23:15)
>
> Woe to you, scribes and Pharisees, hypocrites! For you build the tombs of the prophets and decorate the graves of the righteous, and you say, "If we had lived in the days of our ancestors, we would not have taken part with them in shedding the blood of the prophets." Thus you testify against yourselves that you are descendants of those who murdered the prophets. Fill up, then, the measure of your ancestors. You snakes, you brood of vipers! How can you escape being sentenced to *gehenna*. (Matt 23:33)

I find nothing in these passages that changes the meaning of gehenna from Jeremiah or Isaiah 66:24, as an above-ground burial place where worms and fire decompose the bodies. Note again, however, that our current Bibles (King James, New International Version, New Revised Standard Version) all translate gehenna as hell which implies a totally different meaning.

## HADES IN MATTHEW AND LUKE

Hades is mentioned once in Matthew, twice in Luke. In Matthew 11:23 and Luke 10:15 both are using a common text from Q. "Woe to you, Chorazin! Woe to you, Bethsaida! For if the wonders performed in you had taken place in Tyre and Sidon, they would have repented long ago, in sackcloth and ashes. Yet for Tyre and Sidon it shall be more bearable at the judgment than for you. And you, Capernaum, up to heaven will you be exalted? Into Hades shall you come down!" (Q 10:13–15)

The Q text, "Into Hades you shall come down," is taken from Isaiah 14:14–15, which uses the term Sheol. "But you are brought down to *Sheol*, to the depths of the Pit." We need to remember what Timothy Luke Johnson states, that when the Hebrew texts were translated into the Greek Septuagint the term hades is the equivalent to the Hebrew Sheol.[1] In this passage Jesus' contrast is that Capernaum will not be exalted, but at the end of history it will be brought down to a destruction more severe than was Sodom in Genesis 19:24, when the Lord "rained sulfur and fire from heaven upon Sodom and Gomorrah." This Q passage fits the Hebrew concept of Sheol, not the Greek hades as the deep underground place of eternal punishment.

Luke 16:19–31 is a separate parable wherein human values are reversed by Jesus. In narrating this parable for the Gentile churches, Luke would have been using the Greek Septuagint and thus his use of hades has the meaning of Sheol. In the parable, the rich man was not sympathetic to poor Lazarus. He left Lazarus begging at the gate with the dogs licking his sores. Both died. The rich man, expecting to end in a glory fitting his wealthy position, found himself in hades (Sheol). But Lazarus was carried to Abraham in heaven, thus reversing all normal expectations. In the parable the rich man is a living, seeing, talking entity that can look up to see Abraham with Lazarus. The parable is used to illustrate a point using parabolic language, not factual historical events. The rich man also died and

---

1. Johnson, *Gospel of Luke*, 168.

was buried. In hades (Sheol), where he was being tormented, he looked up and saw Abraham far away with Lazarus by his side. He called out, "Father Abraham, have mercy on me, and send Lazarus to dip the tip of his finger in water and cool my tongue; for I am in agony in these flames" (Luke 16:23).

This is a parable, not a factual statement. The irony of the parable is that the one who did not show mercy now requests mercy. In each of the texts we have been examining, the Greek hades is used as the equivalent to the Hebrew Sheol. We are not dealing with a factual punishing underground hell as implied in our current translations.

## ETERNAL PUNISHMENT IN MATTHEW 25

What does seem clear is that in Matthew 25:31-46, when all the nations are gathered before Jesus, he will separate people from one another as a shepherd separates the sheep from the goats, the just and the unjust. In this passage there is eternal punishment for the unjust. "Then he will answer them, 'Truly I tell you, just as you did not do it to one of the least of these, you did not do it to me.' And these will go away into eternal punishment, but the righteous into eternal life" (Matt 25:46).

But we must note that Matthew was writing for the Jewish Christians and making sharp contrasts between the old religion of the Pharisees and the new religion centered on Jesus. We see this clearly in Matthew's judgment against the scribes and Pharisees calling them "blind guides of the blind" in 15:14 and the harsh series of woes against them in chapter 23. The scribes and Pharisees were certainly the "goats" of this Matthew 25 passage. Matthew, more than any other gospel, uses parallels with the harsh apocalyptic 1 Enoch which are far too close to be dismissed. It was in 1 Enoch 103:7-8 where we saw the concept of Sheol turned into a mythical place of flaming fire and eternal punishment. Matthew parallels 1 Enoch here in his condemnations of those who did not minister to the hungry, or thirsty, or a stranger, or naked, or sick, or in prison, and who "will go away to eternal punishment, but the righteous into eternal life" (Matt 25:46).

It is primarily in Matthew, far more than we see in Jesus or Paul, where we see this harsh view against the Pharisees which he uses to castigate them into eternal punishment. This passage is unique to Matthew. It does not reflect Jesus' words of loving one's enemy or "Father, forgive them for they do not know what they do." In separating the two groups, Matthew is different from Paul's goal of reconciling all of humanity unto God. Thus, I take this particular passage as Matthew adding his own interpretation of Jesus' words to make his own condemnation of the post-70 CE Pharisees. It must be remembered that after the destruction of Jerusalem, the major group left was the Pharisees who were cooperating with the dreaded Roman authorities. Since only the Pharisees believed that the souls of bad men are subject to eternal punishment, was Matthew using the Pharisees' own beliefs of punishment back against them? I believe this is so.

## HADES IN JOHN

The Gospel of John, which was written thirty years after the destruction of Jerusalem, makes no mention of hades, gehenna, nor an eternal punishment. In John 5:29, Jesus mentions a "resurrection to life" and a "resurrection to condemnation" as in Daniel 12. And in John 6:40 there is a resurrection on the last day of those who believe in Jesus. "This is indeed the will of my Father, that all who see the Son and believe in him may have eternal life; and I will raise them up on the last day" (John 6:40).

This passage appears to indicate a significant shift is made by John. The judgment will be based on a theological belief in Jesus, not on criminal acts or other evils that we have seen as the basis of judgment in past, including the failure to have compassion as in Matthew's judgment of the sheep and goats. We see John's shift again in 12:47–48:

> Then Jesus cried aloud: "Whoever believes in me believes not in me but in him who sent me And whoever sees me sees him who sent me. I have come as light into the world, so that everyone who believes in me should not remain in the darkness. I do not judge anyone who hears my words and does not keep them, for I came not to judge the world, but to save the world. The one who rejects me and does not receive my word has a judge; on the last day the word that I have spoken will serve as judge."

This shift from evil actions to a failure of belief in Jesus becomes one of the key markers for salvation by Christians throughout later generations. However, in John the nonbeliever would remain in "darkness." This implies Sheol more than a hades or Tatarus. I feel this is John's attempt to make a sharp division between the believing Christian, and the so-called unbelieving Jews or pagans during the chaotic period following the destruction of temple that we saw in chapter 15. Bernstein indicates that for John,

> the structure of this system is very similar to Paul's, although the terminology is somewhat different. John uses "judgment" where Paul tended to use "wrath," though "wrath" is not foreign to John. The biggest contrast is that John is free of Paul's earlier hesitation about any mention of those who fail in the divine scrutiny. John's position is the solution that Paul arrived at only gradually. John's formula can be stripped to the barest essentials. The judgment by the Son on the authority of the Father will yield eternal life for those who believe, but judgment, wrath, death for those who do not.
>
> This is not a theory of eternal punishment. The wrath of God is expressed as a denial of eternal life. As in Paul, there is no reference to what the content of that death may be. It is "mere" death.[2]

Nothing more is defined, and nothing is said in John about a punishing hell for those who do not believe.

## CONCLUSIONS

It is clear to me that gehenna was for Jesus the valley outside Jerusalem where dead animals, bodies of criminals and others who opposed Yahweh were thrown to be eaten by worms and burnt by the refuse fires. Jesus, knowing the difference between Sheol, gehenna, and the Greek hades, consciously used gehenna. There are two points that are confusing to the contemporary reader. First, as stated before, when the gospels were translated, the Greek Septuagint used hades for Sheol that carried the implication of Plato's hell. Second, gehenna has been mistranslated in English versions as hell in the King James, in the New Revised Standard Version, and in the New International Version. This is misleading.

The terms of Sheol, hades, and Tartarus are clearly mythic in their origin. Unfortunately, in the early church these terms change and became concepts of hell as an actual geographical location. This implies a literal place of punishment by a punitive God using violence to destroy violence. This contradicts the nature of the compassionate, endlessly caring, and forgiving Creator-God we have consistently seen in the Hebrew canon, in Paul, and will see next in the gospels. The concept of gehenna, as a real above-ground Jerusalem valley, the final disgraceful judgment of criminals

---

2. Bernstein, *Formation of Hell*, 225–26.

and those deemed wicked, is more consistent with what Jesus said. Justice is still served.

But we must also put concepts of Tartarus, hades, and hell to the test of current science. Given what we now know about the geology of the earth's surface and its underground composition, none of these three mythic terms can be sustained scientifically as underground storage locations for billions of dead souls and places of fire, worms, and everlasting punishment for the wicked. If there is a place of punishment for the unjust, however they are defined, it cannot be underground within our earth nor within our solar system as we now know it.

Again, we must touch base with the concepts of myth. They are metaphorical constructs, using extremely limited knowledge and language attempting to explain the world as people then experienced it. The biblical people used the myths and terms they knew from their culture. We honor their understandings for their time period. However, the expansion of knowledge, science, and historical insight leave their myths of a punitive God severely wanting. The myth of hell is no longer sustainable except as an instrument of fear in the hands of offended people who want their enemies punished eternally.

If a major task of Jesus' ministry is to make God transparent to humanity, then we need to turn next to passages in the gospels and in Paul where we see this happening.

# 19

# The Nature of the Creator-God

THE ULTIMATE QUESTION OF this work is about the nature of the Creator-God we worship. We have already seen the compassion of Yahweh in the Hebrew canon. We have also seen in chapter 17 both Paul's and John's conviction that the fullness of God dwelt in Jesus and he came to make God known (Col 1:19 and John 1:18). If their theology is correct, then the compassion of God expressed in the Hebrew canon passages should become transparent in all that Jesus said and did. It has been my personal conviction that if we wish to know what our Creator-God is like we look to Jesus Christ. If we wish to know what human beings should be like we also look to Jesus Christ. If we wish to know what humans too often have become like we look at his killing on the cross.

## THE NATURE OF GOD IN JESUS

Jesus' early ministry was in rural Galilee to the simple peasants who had suffered extreme hardship over the prior centuries, as we have already seen. They were mostly illiterate and did not know all the refinements of the written and oral law. Thus they were seen by the priestly elite of Jerusalem as beyond redemption. It was to these rural outsiders that Jesus began his ministry.

In his messages to them Jesus reverses the historical exclusion of these people and compassionately includes them. This was the greatest news these peasant people could ever hear, for it was a reversal of what they had

## The Nature of the Creator-God

ever heard from the priests of Jerusalem with their laws of exclusion. In Q, Jesus says to all those who had been cast aside as beyond God's care, that they are now included in God's love and protection. This element of compassion is seen time and again and is one of the key signatures of Jesus' healing ministry to these peasants. There is no punitive anger from God in these messages, only compassion and inclusiveness.

We also see compassion in many of the acts of Jesus. We see it in the healing of a man with so-called unclean spirits, in the healing of the untouchable leper, in the healing and forgiveness of the paralytic lowered down though the roof, in Jesus eating with the sinners and tax collectors, in breaking restrictive laws by healing the man with the withered hand on the sabbath, in the healing of Jairus' daughter and the woman with the hemorrhage, in the healings of the Syrophoenician's daughter, the blind man at the Bathsaida well, the deaf, and the epileptic child. These were the blemished people who were cast aside by the Levitical laws of uncleanness. Jesus' compassionate ministry reversed these Levitical laws and included these outsiders inside God's love and healing protection. Again, these acts of Jesus shows a Creator-God of profound compassion to the very people who had been excluded by priestly practices for centuries. We see no punitive God in these actions.

In the earliest of Jesus' sayings in Q we find Jesus' statement to love one's enemies (Q 6:27), in the Lord's Prayer for God's kingdom to come on earth (Q 11:2b), in the parables of the mustard seed and yeast concerning the growth of the kingdom (Q 13:18–19), and in the statement that the kingdom is among you (Q 17:20–21). We see God's searching out the lost sheep and lost coin (Q 15:4–5a, 15:8–10), the woes against the powerful and the elite Pharisees and scribes (Q 11:39–44, 11:46–48), and the beatitudes for the poor, the hungry, the persecuted (Q 6:20–23). These each show God's nature through the transparency of Jesus.

In Luke we are given even more understanding of God's nature in Jesus. Luke includes Mary's Magnificat and its visions for Jesus' mission to take down the powerful and send the rich away empty, but to lift up and fill the lowly and the hungry (Luke 1:51–55). Luke adds to his gospel the parables of the Good Samaritan with the hero being a rejected Samaritan to whom no respectable Jew would talk (Luke 10:29–37); and the parable of the Prodigal Son where the father (God) runs out to eagerly greet the returning sinful son and throws a celebration party (15:11–32). It is also in Luke that we hear Jesus' most gracious words to the very people killing him, "Father, forgive them for they do not know what they are doing" (Luke 23:34). If part of Jesus' ministry is to reveal the fullness of God, these actions are powerful word-pictures of a deeply compassionate Creator-God.

The writer of Matthew also adds comforting words of Jesus which must have been welcomed by the beleaguered peasants: "Come to me, all you that are weary and are carrying heavy burdens, and I will give you rest. Take my yoke upon you, and learn from me; for I am gentle and humble in heart, and you will find rest for your souls. For my yoke is easy, and my burden is light" (Matt 11:28). Matthew includes Jesus' use of Isaiah 42 that indicates a servant role for Jesus, not the rule of an imperialistic king. It was also in Isaiah 42 that we saw the Servant's role as a teacher, a designation picked up again and again in the gospels where people addressed Jesus as a teacher.

Thus in these first reports of Jesus' ministry we find the Son of God acting out the nature and personality of the one he saw as his Father, all of which shows a compassionate, reconciling and teaching concern toward those previously deemed as outside of God's care. Jesus' anger, and thus God's, was directed toward those who treated these outsiders with contempt. Here Jesus reverses the whole social and religious structure of the status quo.

John and the early church came to the conviction that the Word that was God from the beginning of creation took on human flesh and dwelled among humanity. Jesus was the Word who came to humanity to make the Creator-God fully known. It is clear to the writer of John that what one sees in Jesus *is* the inner nature of the Creator-God. We can point to a variety of passages. beginning with John 3:16–17 and John 12:46–47:

> For God so loved the world that he gave his only Son, so that everyone who believes in him may not perish but may have eternal life. Indeed, God did not send the Son into the world to condemn the world, but in order that the world might be saved [reconciled] through him. (3:16–17)
> 
> I have come as light into the world, so that everyone who believes in me should not remain in the darkness. I do not judge anyone who hears my words and does not keep them, for I came not to judge the world, but to save [reconcile] the world. (12:46–47)

We can add to that from John: Jesus speaking to the Samaritan woman at the well, an act of inclusion which no law-abiding Jew would have done (4:7–26); Jesus' forgiving the woman accused of adultery to the

## The Nature of the Creator-God

astonishment of the scribes and Pharisees (8:1–11); his giving the commandment of love in both 13:34–35 and 15:12–17; and in 17:24–26 Jesus is showing the same love to humanity which God had shown to him. John's understanding of the Creator-God contains no angry, punitive aspect. As Yahweh heard the slaves in Egypt and bent down to released them from bondage, God in Jesus heard the cries of his people and bent down to free them from the bondage of restrictive laws, from the control of a corrupted priesthood, and from the oppression of the Romans. The Creator-God seen in Jesus is loving, reconciling, and restorative.

We have seen in Paul, and now in the gospels, that the God seen transparent in Jesus continues to be the compassionate Yahweh of the Hebrew canon, yearning to love and heal a broken humanity. This is the nature of the Creator-God who is behind the whole universe. There is no punitive God here.

What is striking in a sequential reading of Mark, Luke, and Matthew is that we see little, if any, of the apocalyptic images used by Jesus. Here I find myself still in agreement with my New Testament professor at the San Francisco Theological Seminary of years ago, Dr. John Wick Bowman, who taught that Jesus stood in the Hebrew prophetic tradition and had nothing in common with the apocalyptic myths.[1] I find myself reaffirmed in this decision after reading the discussion of recent scholars in Robert Miller's *Apocalyptic Jesus: A Debate*. I do not see in Jesus a God of violence who will murder all humanity as those who do not act or believe correctly, as in the apocalyptic literature. I do not see in Jesus images of God using violence to destroy violence. What I do see is a compassionate Creator-God who, in Jesus, is fighting human systemic evil and yearning to love and reconcile all humanity within a history that will continue for ages.

If these conclusions are correct, where did things go off track and punitive concepts of hell and Satan become fixed dogma? For the response to this question we must turn next to the early church fathers and their writings.

---

1. Bowman, *Intention of Jesus*, 52.

# 20

# An Unsettled Christendom

## CHRISTIAN CANON FORMATION

IT IS IMPORTANT FOR us to realize how unsettled these first Christian centuries were. There was no consensus on what composed the Christian canon. As early as 139 CE, Marcion developed a Christian Bible with only the Gospel of Luke and the ten Pauline Letters but nothing else. The early Christians were already seeing Paul's Letters as scriptural. But Marcion rejected the Hebrew canon, and the early Church rejected Marcion as being too gnostic–beliefs that we will look at shortly. Justin, in ca. 153 CE, was convinced that the Hebrew canon was essential for religious history as an infallible revelation of the Messiah to come and the foundation for understanding Jesus. This was the first bid for an infallible Old Testament. The early Church rejected Justin because he was antagonistic toward Judaism and he simply ignored Paul's writings. Tatian, in ca. 160 CE, tried to make one blended gospel out of the four gospels. But he left out all of Jesus' birth stories. The Bishop Dionysius of Alexandria, in 200 CE, said the book of Revelation was not written by John, nor is it a revelation, and certainly not to be taken literally. The book of Revelation was the subject of many debates. This is hardly the stuff of a singular Christendom with a common biblical text.

It was not until 387 CE at the Synod of Carthage that the limits of the New Testament were defined as the present twenty-seven books. A crucial figure in the formation of our modern Bible was historian and theologian

Jerome (ca. 347–420 CE), a scholar in Greek, Latin, and some Hebrew. It was he who developed the Latin Vulgate text from original Hebrew texts. Prior to this the church and Greek-speaking Christians had accepted the Septuagint as the only reliable translation. But we must remember that the Septuagint had translated the Hebrew Sheol into the Greek hades, changing its meaning from a nonpunitive concept to a step toward punishment. In the Vulgate, Jerome consistently translated the original Hebrew Sheol into the Latin *infernum*. The Douay-Rheims Bible of the Roman church, based on the Vulgate, consistently translated *infernum* as hell. Where Jerome had consistently retained the gospel's gehenna into the Latin *gehennam*, the Douay-Rheims texts also translated *gehennam* as hell. This means all early Christians, whether using the Septuagint or the Vulgate version, were reading the nonpunitive Hebrew terms of Sheol and gehenna incorrectly as an eternally punishing hell.

## A FIERY HELL

Given that the early church fathers were reading hell in their Scriptures, it appears that many of them picked up the Targum on Isaiah 66:24, the gospel's use of gehenna, and Matthew's 25:41, and congealed them together into an underground hades of unquenchable fire and eternal punishment. A series of their statements are as follows. Note that part of Irenaeus of Lyons' statement is a direct quote from Matthew 25:41.

- Justin Martyr, 150 CE: "We have been taught that only they may aim at immortality who have lived a holy and virtuous life near to God. We believe that they who live wickedly and do not repent will be punished in everlasting fire" (*First Apology*, 21).
- Irenaeus of Lyons, 189 CE: "The penalty increases for those who do not believe the Word of God and despise his coming. . . . It is not merely temporal, but eternal. To whomsoever the Lord shall say, 'Depart from me, accursed ones, into the everlasting fire,' they will be damned forever" (*Against Heresies*, 4:28:2).
- Tertullian, 197 CE: "The worshippers of God shall always be with God, clothed in the proper substance of eternity. But the godless and those who have not turned wholly to God will be punished in fire equally unending, and they shall have from the very nature of this fire, divine as it were, a supply of incorruptibility" (*Apology* , 44:12–13).

## Eliminating Satan and Hell

- Hippolytus, 212 CE: "Standing before [Christ's] judgment, all of them, men, angels, and demons, crying out in one voice, shall say: 'Just is your judgment!' And the righteousness of that cry will be apparent in the recompense made to each. To those who have done well, everlasting enjoyment shall be given; while to the lovers of evil shall be given eternal punishment . . . and a certain fiery worm which does not die and which does not waste the body but continually bursts forth from the body with unceasing pain. No sleep will give them rest; no night will soothe them; no death will deliver them from punishment; no appeal of interceding friends will profit them" (*Against the Greeks*, 3).

It clear from these early theologians that during this period there was general descriptive agreement about a punishing, fiery and eternal end for nonbelievers, especially for those who opposed the defined Christian beliefs. It was also a time of competing theologies.

## GNOSTICISM

Gnosticism was a thoroughly dualistic offshoot of late Judaism and early Christianity. There were many adherents who believed themselves as Christians and believed created matter was intrinsically evil. Since evil matter cannot be from God, it must be the result of some primeval disorder, some conflict or fall in the cosmic order. Its creator must have been some inferior deity. Further, since godhood could not associate with evil matter and God cannot be killed, God's spirit could not have been fully embodied in Jesus' human body but only temporarily. Godhood left either before the crucifixion or Jesus never really died and only appeared to do so. Gnosticism believed the world was ruled by evil demons that held humanity in captivity. A belief in the secret knowledge of Gnosticism was thought to set one free from this evil.

Valentinus, who lectured at Alexandria ca. 120 to 140, was a primary proponent of Gnosticism and felt only its members had been enlightened by these secret beliefs. J. N. D. Kelly, principal of St. Edmund Hall, Oxford, England, indicates there was a powerful strain in early Christianity that was in sympathy with gnostic tendencies.[1] However, the early Church rejected Gnosticism as a heresy.

---

1. Kelly, *Early Christian Doctrines*, 27.

*An Unsettled Christendom*

## THE NATURE OF JESUS AND NICAEA

All was not settled about the nature of Jesus the Christ. If the Logos (or Word) of the first chapter of the Gospel of John dwelled fully in Christ, was this from all eternity, or only later, or not at all? Paul of Samosata, the bishop of Antioch (260–268 CE), taught that the Logos of God was an independent reality that remained in heaven apart from the earthly Jesus who was anointed by grace. However, Paul of Samosata was condemned in the church synods of 264 CE and 268 CE. It was the fallout from this teaching that set up vigorous debates between key theologians.

Peter of Alexandria, who was pope of Alexandria (300 to 311 CE), attempted to standardize doctrinal teaching in Alexandria and held that the Son of God is the same essence and substance with the Father and was created by God. However, he was challenged by Arius (ca. 250 to 336 CE), a Christian presbyter in Alexandria, on the difference between God and the Logos. Arius claimed it was the Logos that presided over creation, and is not therefore properly divine but only as the first and greatest of creatures. Since it is this Logos that dwelt in Jesus, Jesus is not of the same substance as is God nor had he dwelt for all eternity. Peter of Alexandria drove the Arians out of the city as heretical.

During this period, Emperor Constantine became deeply disturbed that such theological controversies were splitting his empire between the West and the East and wanted Christianity as a unifying factor in his empire. Therefore, in 325 CE, he called for a council of the church synod in Nicaea to resolve the issues. At the council the two main contestants were Arius and Athanasius, the arch-deacon of Alexandria. The council, supporting Athanasius, rejected Arius, and adopted the Nicene Creed, which affirmed:

> We believe . . . in one Lord Jesus Christ, the Son of God, begotten from the Father, only-begotten, that is, from the substance of the Father, God of God, Light of Light, true God from true God, begotten not made, of one substance with the Father, through Whom all things came into being, things in heaven and on earth.

For an unsettled Christendom, the Nicene Council eventually secured for the Western church the doctrine of the complete oneness of Jesus with the divinity of God. However, if the Nicene Creed secured Jesus' divinity, it was not until 390 CE that the Apostles' Creed secured the humanity of

Jesus in the phrase "born of the Virgin Mary." This left many other issues unsettled, such as Pelagius's view of the nature of the human being.

## PELAGIANISM

Pelagius is thought to have been born in the British Isles about 354 CE. The last he was heard from was 418 CE. A monk of the Celtic Johannine Christian Order, he moved to Rome to write and teach. The most that is known about him comes from followers and critics such as Augustine and Julian of Eclanum. Henry Bettenson indicates that Pelagius believed a good Creator-God would not allow one man's sin to condemn all subsequent humanity, nor would such a God create a baby sinful at birth. He believed evil came from bad human choice and its accumulation in society. He also believed that death is a natural process and not a penalty caused by Adam's sin.[2]

We know today through epigenetic scholars such as Dr. Michael Skinner

> that it is not possible for sin to be inherit genetically from the beginning of humanity down through all following generations. The brain develops from stem cells at each generation, and although the basic structure and capacity is present, passing on thought processes do not. Although we have the capacity for good or evil it is not predetermined or inherited that we have sin. Thus the doctrine of original sin cannot be sustained scientifically.[3]

We also know there is a natural necessity of death for all living creatures. On these particulars Pelagius was on the right path and his condemners were mistaken. But Pelagius and Pelagianism were condemned by the Roman church.

## AUGUSTINE, THE BISHOP OF HIPPO

Augustine was born in Carthage, Algeria, in 354 CE, the son of a poor, uneducated family. He was first a schoolmaster, then a monk, and finally the bishop of Hippo. Eventually, he became the foremost theologian of early

---

2. Bettenson, *Documents of the Christian Church*, 55.

3. Dr. Michael Skinner, professor and director of the Center for Reproductive Biology, School of Molecular Biosciences, Washington State University, Pullman, WA, and an expert in epigenetics, from personal communication.

*An Unsettled Christendom*

Christendom upon whose writings much in the Christian faith became fixed dogma for many centuries to come.

Augustine's Scriptures were primarily the Greek Septuagint and Jerome's Latin Vulgate. In his *City of God against the Pagans*, Augustine wrote:

> The Church has received the Septuagint as if it were the only translation. The Greek-speaking Christian peoples use it, and most of them do not know that there is any other. From this Septuagint a translation into Latin has also been made, to which the Latin-speaking churches adhere. Moreover, in our time has come the Presbyter Jerome, a most learned man and a scholar of all three languages; and he has translated these same Scriptures into Latin, not from the Greek but from the Hebrew.[4]

We have already seen the Septuagint's translation of Sheol into a punitive hades; and Jerome's Vulgate translation of the Hebrew Sheol into the Latin infernum implying a fiery place of eternal punishment. This meant early Christians like Augustine, whether using the Septuagint or the Vulgate version, were reading the nonpunitive Hebrew terms incorrectly as an eternally punishing hell. To be fair to Augustine, he was following the earlier writers we have just seen with their belief in an eternal fiery hell largely based on Mark's 9:42–40 use of the Isaiah 66:24, Targum, and Matthew 25:41, 46. Augustine also accepted Scripture as divinely inspired and founded much of his theology largely on the myth of the garden of Eden in Genesis 2–3, on Romans 5:12, on Psalm 51:5, and the apocalyptic book of Revelation.

## AUGUSTINE ON ADAM IN GARDEN OF EDEN

Augustine felt humans were created to be between the angels and the beasts in such a way that if they had remained obedient to God there would have been no death. He wrote: "If they discharged the duty of obedience, the reward of an angelic immortality and a blessed eternity was to follow without the intervention of death; but if they disobeyed, they were to be most justly punished with the sentence of death."[5]

Augustine misunderstood Genesis 2–3 where the word "Adam" means the whole of humanity. Thus he treats "Adam" as the first human being from

---

4. Augustine, *City of God*, 884.
5. Ibid., 541.

whose rib Eve, as the first woman, was created. Augustine also accepted the garden of Eden paradise myth as a reality, where everything was peaceful, with no death and no evil, and harmoniously joined with God.

> [Adam] lived without any want, and he had it within his power so to live for ever. Food was present, lest he hunger; drink, lest he thirst; and the tree of life, lest age decay him. There was no corruption in the body, or arising from the body, to bring any distress to any of his senses. There was supreme health of body, and entire tranquility of soul . . . there was no extreme of heat or cold in Paradise. . . . There was nothing of sadness; neither was there any empty pleasure. Rather, true joy poured forth continually from God, good conscience, and of faith unfeigned. A faithful fellowship of honest love existed between the pair; there was a concord and alertness of mind and body, and God's commandment was kept without labour. In his leisure, man did not know the weariness of fatigue, and sleep never pressed upon him against his will.[6]

Augustine's first Adam and Eve would have enjoyed paradise, raised a family through sexual intercourse with no "moans of pain" in the birth process, and had they not sinned, would not have died. This makes clear that Augustine built upon the Genesis 2–3 myth but changed Adam and Eve from metaphoric terms into the first humans who were obedient to God in an ideal setting where there was no death, no pain in childbirth, no hard work.

## AUGUSTINE ON ORIGINAL SIN

Scholars indicate that it was Turtullian who first said that Adam knew what he was doing and chose freely; since his fall, sin has acquired natural status and corruption is passed from every parent to every child. Augustine picked this up in his theology. Augustine believed so strongly in the ideal garden, that the only way to explain evil was that something tragically wrong had happened to cause a "fall" for which God had to place a curse upon humanity. Augustine treated Genesis 2–3 as a reality and not a myth and blamed the mythic Adam for the tragic fall.

He knew his early life was not free from sin, especially since he had a concubine for many years before his marriage. In combing the Old Testament for scriptural authority, Augustine found Psalm 51:5. "Indeed I was

---

6. Ibid., 628–29.

born guilty, a sinner when my mother conceived me." He built upon this passage the conclusion that from Adam, on down all history, human beings are genetically born sinful. This was the basis for his claiming that babies are born with sin that needed to be washed away with baptism. Augustine wrote:

> We must, then, confess that the first human beings were so constituted that, had they not sinned, they would not have experienced any kind of death; but that, having become the first sinners, they were then punished by death in such a way that whatsoever sprang from their stock should also be subject to the same penalty. For nothing could be born of them which was not what they themselves had been. Their nature was changed for the worse in proportion to the condemnation attaching to the magnitude of their sin, so that what arose as a punishment in the first human beings who sinned also follows as a natural consequence in the rest who are born of them.
>
> But man the parent is the same thing as man the offspring. In the first man, therefore, there existed the whole human race that was to pass through the woman into her progeny when that conjugal pair received the divine sentence of its own damnation. And what man became, not when he was created, but when he sinned and was punished: this he propagated, so far as the origin of sin and death are concerned. He himself was not reduced by sin or its punishment to that infantile condition and helpless weakness of mind and body that we see in little children. But God ordained that infants should henceforth be like the young of beasts in their origin, since their parents had fallen to the level of the beasts in the manner of their life and death.[7]

But we have already seen above that original sin is a doctrine that can no longer be sustained scientifically.

## AUGUSTINE ON THE DEVIL (SATAN)

Augustine was a firm believer in the creation of angels of light before the creation of humanity.[8] He believed the devil was first created without flesh as an angel of light. If he had remained loyal to God he would have remained in blessedness with the angels. However, the devil chose to live "according

---

7. Ibid., 543–44.
8. Ibid., 466.

to self when he did not abide in the truth, so that the lie that he told was his own, and not God's. The devil is not only a liar, he is 'the father of lies': he was indeed, the first to lie, and falsehood, like sin, began with him."[9] It was this rebellious angel, then, who

> sought to insinuate himself, by crafty suggestion, into the heart of man, whose unfallen state he envied now that he himself had fallen. To this end, he chose to speak through a serpent in the corporeal Paradise where the other earthly animals dwelt, tame and harmless, with the two human beings, the male and the female; and this creature, slippery and moving in twisting coils, was indeed well suited to such work. By virtue of his angelic stature and his superior nature, Satan made the serpent subject to him in spiritual wickedness, and, by abusing it as his instrument, had deceitful converse with the woman.[10]

In our chapter 4 we saw the biblical serpent was one of God's good creation who simply voiced to humanity that God had given humans a freedom of choice for obedience or rebellion. Augustine changed this and made the serpent a voice of Satan. By Augustine's time, the Hebrew concept of hassatan as one of Yahweh's good agents had become the concept of Satan, the enemy of God and humanity. Augustine's reality of Satan became the dogma of the church.

## AUGUSTINE ON BIRTH, DEATH, RESURRECTION, AND CONDEMNATION

Augustine's understanding of birth and death is complex and comes into play here. He believed that at birth, God, by breathing into the body, either places the soul into the human body or God's breath is the soul being place in the body.[11] At death, the breath of God stops and the soul departs the dead body. The first resurrection then is of the soul, not the body.[12] This is a resurrection of mercy where the souls of the righteous raise up and will be blessed for all eternity. There is a second resurrection of judgment where the bodies of the unrighteous will be hurled into condemnation and shall die a second death. After the second resurrection, sinful humans with

9. Ibid., 586.
10. Ibid., 605–6.
11. Ibid., 534–35.
12. Ibid., 978.

bodies and demons without bodies, can live and remain alive forever in Augustine's "lake of fire and brimstone." To those who question whether the dead can be burned, Augustine answers: "I have now sufficiently discussed the question of whether it is possible, for living creatures to remain alive even in fire. And I have shown that by a miracle of their most omnipotent Creator, they can burn without being consumed, and suffer without dying. Anyone who denies that this is possible does not understand Who brings about everything in nature that amazes him."[13]

For those who ask if the devil and the wicked will be punished eternally, he answers: "Because the eternal life of the saints will be without end, there is no doubt that the eternal punishment of those condemned to it will also have no end."[14] For Augustine, since all humanity is infected with sin from birth, all will be punished with eternal fire unless one is either baptized and/or made a confession of faith in Christ.[15]

## AUGUSTINE ON THE GRACE OF GOD

Pelagius had felt that God created in humanity the freedom of choice. He looked to Deuteronomy 30:19, "I have set before you life and death, blessings and curses. Choose life that you and your descendants may live." This implied for Pelagius that humanity always retained the capacity to make a choice for good or evil, for God or against God, and it depended upon the individual Hebrew to make that choice.

However, Augustine was convinced that no matter how strenuously "we repel our vices, and no matter how successful we are in overcoming and subduing them, for as long as we remain in this body we can never be without reason for saying to God, 'Forgive us our trespasses.'"[16] With his doctrine of original sin from Adam, Augustine felt humans are helpless to make that choice and stand condemned. Only by God's grace can a choice for God be made.

This opens the question: to whom will God's grace be given? I don't really find Augustine's answer. He asks: "What, then, will those rewards be, if the consolations are so many and so great? What will God give to those whom He has predestined to life, if He has given all these things even to

13. Ibid., 1069.
14. Ibid., 1084.
15. Ibid., 1076.
16. Ibid., 1158.

those predestined to death?"[17] And here we stumble into predestination. Peter Brown, Princeton professor of history, indicates that the "doctrine of predestination was developed by Augustine mainly as a doctrine in which every event was charged with a precise meaning as a deliberate act of God, of mercy for the elect, of judgment for the damned."[18] This gave great confidence to those who claimed they were part of "an unshakable number of the elect." But it was terror for everybody else. Since even those who had made a decision for Christ and been baptized were still sinners, they could not be certain. There is no answer as to whom God will elect for the glories of resurrection.

On May 1, 418, the Council of Carthage, with the presence of two hundred bishops, condemned Pelagianism as a heresy and gave it a deathblow. This led to the establishment of Augustine as the prince of the church's theologians. Unfortunately, it also established his doctrines of Satan, hell and original sin, among others, to be articles of faith binding on the Western church.

In this chapter we have seen the separation of Christianity from Judaism and also from Roman and Greek paganism. It was a time of discussion, debate and striking differences as the emerging Christian community attempted to define its essential Christian doctrine. Too often, those of one theological position were quick to castigate those of opposing positions as agents of Satan needing to be consigned into the fiery darkness of hell. Thus the apocalyptic myths of Satan and hell were recalled and continued in their use then and even to this day.

## CONCLUSIONS

What has been transparent in this whole study is that concepts of Satan and hell are mythical. Ancient populations were very conscious of evil: the evil of occupying nations, the evil of economic exploitation, the evil of personal enemies and their vendettas. It was important for those populations that a level of justice operate with rewards for the righteous (however defined) and a punishment for their wicked enemies (however defined). As we have seen, the myth of a Satan was developed to explain for them the cause of evil. The myth of hell was developed to justify for them that their enemies would be punished. The myth of angry gods, or an angry God, to carry out

17. Ibid., 1165.
18. Brown, *Augustine of Hippo*, 407.

the punishment was part of the package. The early church and theologians like Augustine bought into these myths and used them to encourage their supporters and condemn their opponents.

However, as we have seen, the Jewish community never bought into the myths of a personal Satan as an enemy of God, nor a hell as a place of eternal punishment. As we have also seen, neither Paul nor Jesus of the gospels bought into these apocalyptic myths of a retributive God. Given what we now know of our universe, of our physical earth, of the evolution of humanity, and the composition of each person, the myths of Satan and hell are empty and no longer have legitimate substance as valid explanations of our current world. Our theologies must recognize this and change.

# 21

# Postscript

WE HAVE SEEN THAT ancient myths gave meaning to the reality people were then experiencing based on the vastly limited knowledge of the world about them. The myths of Satan, Azazel, Mastemah, Belial served as the causes of evil. The myths of hades and Tartarus served as a place of punishment for those whom the Greeks and the Jewish apocalypticists saw as evil. When the people's knowledge expanded and the myths no longer worked they developed new theological understandings.

Likewise, our theologies must change by owning up to two problems: First, as seen in the research for this book, we have remained locked into the theology of the early church fathers without realizing that their theologies departed from the theology of the Hebrew canon, of Paul, and of Jesus. Second, it is also clear that the myths of Satan and hell have been carried over into our theologies without facing up to the greatly expanded scientific knowledge we now embrace.

For our contemporary theologies, we must take into consideration the discoveries of: (a) the Hubble telescope for the age, the vastness, and awesomeness of our universe; (b) the findings of the Swiss-based Hadron Collider about the beginning of creation, as explained by Harvard University's Lisa Randall[1]; (c) the complexity of DNA for what is inheritable and what is not; and (d) the history and nature of humanity, as traced by such authors as Ian Tattersall, a curator in the American Museum of Natural History,[2]

1. Randall, *Knocking at Heaven's Door*.
2. Tattersall, *Masters of the Planet*.

*Postscript*

and the world-renown biologist and naturalist Edward O. Wilson.[3] The wisdom of these writers and many others, are only a few of the learnings that we must embrace to calculate into our theologies.

While I have concluded from my research that the myths of Satan, hell, original sin, and others no longer have reality as valid explanations for our current world, we must still acknowledge the reality of evil. This must be confronted within the confines of our current knowledge, not from yesterday's myths. A systematic exploration of evil is both part of this work, but also beyond its scope for that would require a whole new book. However, there are several parameters that such a book should cover.

First, the Creator-God behind our universe does not create evil. Evil does not come from outside our planet, but from within our earthly human community. We are our own Adams, our own Eves, and are responsible for evil.

Second, not all that we sometimes call evil is evil. Within the mechanics of our earth there are tragedies from neutral forces of nature: earthquakes, major storms, floods, droughts, famines, etc. These can be painfully tragic. But they are not evil in the sense that some personalized force is trying to hurt people. These are not vengeful vendettas of the gods. Therefore, it is not fair to ask, "Why did God let such a tragedy happen?" any more than to blame God when the winds blow, or floods and hurricanes come, or the earth's tectonic plates shift. These are not evil actions.

Third, there are personal actions people do out of spite, jealousy, reactions to a sense of injustice, etc. Personal reactions are then involved all the way from demanding an apology to getting revenge by murder. At some level, codified laws begin to operate to declare certain actions as illegal, and defined punishments are administered. Our whole legal system is based on the fact that people are answerable for what they do. Such actions are usually defined as legal or illegal, but not necessarily evil.

Fourth, there is another level where systems are created to gain certain benefits for those in power, but end up controlling, enslaving or impoverishing others. We saw this in the *Enuma Elish* myth where humans were created to serve the gods. Concepts such as divine right of kings, warlords, and dictatorships such as in Nazism and Communism fit this category. Usually seen in these systems is the silencing or extermination of opposition populations, political or religious. In these systems Lord Acton's dictum is correct: "Power tends to corrupt and absolute power tends to corrupt

---

3. Wilson, *Social Conquest of Earth*.

absolutely." The citizens are denied instruments of power and are helpless to change the systems. We saw during the Greek period of occupation of Israel where such systems were so overpowering that the names of Satan, Azazel, Mastemah, Belial were given to personalize evil. The people could only pray for God to step in with a Savior to create a whole new heaven and a new earth. The proper adjective to call such dehumanizing systems is "evil."

However, we must recognize that such evil systems may be perfectly legal. Hitler probably broke no German laws in the extermination of six million Jews and communists in pursuit of German unity and the purity of an Aryan race. Stalin probably broke no Soviet laws in his state liquidation of opposition groups. Yet, both actions were evil. We must recognize that many who endorsed such systems were basically good people in almost all other respects because in their minds the ends justified the means. Many of those who carried out monstrous acts were probably good citizens, good fathers and loving husbands who were simply carrying out orders. Terry Eagleton, professor of English literature at the National University of Ireland, Galway, observes that

> those who steal pension funds or pollute whole regions of the planet are quite often mild-mannered individuals who believe that business is business . . . the point is that most wickedness is institutional. It is the result of vested interests and anonymous processes, not of the maligned acts of individuals. . . . For the most part, however, such outrages are the product of particular systems. . . . Because most forms of wickedness are built into our social systems, the individuals who serve those systems may well be unaware of the gravity of their actions . . . many individuals who act in politically obnoxious ways are sensitive, conscientious men and women who believe they are selflessly serving the state, the company, God, or the future of the Free world.[4]

We can identify many systemic attitudes and actions today, such as nationalism, racism, militarism, favoring the rich and powerful while ignoring the poor and the suffering, etc., that are held in the hearts of many in the world, which may not be illegal, but are certainly evil in the destruction of individuals and societies. We have already mentioned McLean and Cocera's book, where a greed swept like slime over Wall Street in the late American recession and caused tragic financial loss and pain for millions

---

4. Eagleton, *On Evil*, 143–44.

around the world, but which seems to have broken no laws. The authors' comment:

> It is very hard to find the line between delusion, venality, and outright corruption. Much of what took place during the crisis was immoral, unjust, craven, delusional behavior—but it wasn't criminal. The most clear-cut cases of corruption—the broker who tricked people into bad mortgages, the Wall Street bankers who knowingly packaged mortgages—are in the shadows, cogs inside the wheels like Ameriquest, New Century, Merrill Lynch, and Goldman Sachs. We'll probably never even learn most of those people's names.[5]

Many of those involved may have been in churches every Sunday feeling justified that they were simply doing a good job of what the company needed. But was not this caused by evil greed operating within a social system? It is this that I have been calling "systemic evil," which mythic terms are no longer adequate to identify.

One of the challenges before us is to explore quickly and sharply the ways of identifying attitudes and actions that benefit us today, but foreclose or destroy life for future generations and therefore end up being systemically evil. To use examples: the future of earth's environment. We each, as law-abiding people who would injure no one, enjoy the benefits of today's coal and gasoline for our comfort and travel which in reality may be tragically crippling the environment of future generations. Will our attitudes and actions be judged by those ten, twenty, fifty generations down the path of history as having been systemically non-caringly indulgent and thus evil? Is our consumerism and throw-away society thoughtlessly using up earth's resources that will be desperately needed by future generations and, again, be seen by future generations as evil on our part?

For us to continue to retain the myths of a cosmic Satan, who is beyond human reach, as the responsible agent for evil is to deny the biblical truth that evil is human caused. It is ours to own and ours is the responsibility to confront it within our human systems. To retain the myth of hell as a place of eternal punishment is also to deny the biblical truth of a compassionate God and assign to God the tyrannical role of using evil to punish the evil to justify our sense of justice. To retain the myth of original sin is not only to deny the goodness of the Creator in the newborn, but also the goodness

---

5. McLean and Nocera, *All the Devils Are Here*, 362.

## Eliminating Satan and Hell

we see in our fellow human beings. It also denies the science of DNA that sin cannot be inherited.

It seems to me that the tasks of the theologian, the politician, the scientist, the common citizen is to be collaborating on where in our social, economic, political systems we are fostering systemic evil that will haunt generations down the road. We know the Creator-God began this universe some 13.5 billions years ago and we began to inhabit the earth some 4.5 billion years ago. Creation talks in term of billions and millions of years, not in terms of generations. The scientist-theologian John Polkinghorne, past president of Queens' College, Cambridge, suggests that in about five billion years the sun's hydrogen core will be exhausted and burn out.[6] This leaves us to ask how many thousands of years humans may yet have to live on our earth? What resources need we be saving, what social systems need we be building that respects the survivability of humanity to share the earth together? What systems of evil are we now fostering economically, politically, geographically that will cripple or bankrupt the future?

In face of these questions, the myths of Satan and hell no longer work and are empty! They give us no leverage by which to address the pressing issues of systemic evil within our world. They are vindictive, destructive, and an insult to the magnificence of our compassionate Creator-God. It may be difficult to erase these terms from our vocabularies, but we must at least change our theologies.

---

6. Polkinghorne, *God of Hope*, 8.

# Bibliography

Ackroyd, Peter. *Exile and Restoration: A Study of Hebrew Thought of the Sixth Century B.C.* Old Testament Library. Philadelphia: Westminster, 1968.
Albright, W. F., and C. S. Mann. *Matthew*. Anchor Bible. Garden City: Doubleday, 1971.
Anderson, Bernhard W. *Understanding the Old Testament*. 3rd ed. Englewood Cliffs, NJ: Prentice Hall, 1975.
Anderson, Bernhard W., and Walter Harrelson. *Israel's Prophetic Heritage: Essays in Honor of James Muilenburg.* London: SCM, 1962.
Armstrong, Karen. *The Battle for God: A History of Fundamentalism.* New York: Random House, 2000.
———. *A History of God: The 4000-Year Quest of Judaism, Christianity and Islam.* New York: Ballantine, 1993.
———. *A Short History of Myth.* New York: Cannongate, 2005.
Augustine. *The City of God against the Pagans.* Edited by R. W. Dyson. Cambridge: Cambridge University Press, 1998.
Baker, Sharon L. *Razing Hell: Rethinking Everything You've Been Taught about God's Wrath and Judgment.* Louisville: Westminster John Knox, 2010.
Bell, Rob. *Love Wins: A Book about Heaven, Hell, and the Fate of Every Person Who Ever Lived.* New York: HarperCollins, 2011.
Bernstein, Alan E. *The Formation of Hell: Death and Retribution in Ancient and Early Christian Worlds.* Ithaca: Cornell University Press, 1993.
Bettenson, Henry. *Documents of the Christian Church.* New York: Oxford University Press, 1947.
Borg, Marcus J., and N. T. Wright. *The Meaning of Jesus: Two Visions.* San Francisco: HarperSanFrancisco, 1999.
Bowman, John Wick. *The Intention of Jesus.* Philadelphia: Westminster, 1943.
Boyce, Mary. *Textual Sources for the Study of Zoroastrianism.* Chicago: University of Chicago Press, 1990.
———. *Zoroastrians: Their Religious Beliefs and Practices.* London: Routledge, 1979.
Brown, Peter. *Augustine of Hippo: A Biography.* Berkeley: University of California Press, 2000.
Brueggemann, Walter. *Genesis.* Interpretation. Atlanta: John Knox, 1982.
———. *An Introduction to the Old Testament: The Canon and Christian Imagination.* Louisville: Westminster John Knox, 2003.
———. *An Unsettling God: The Heart of the Hebrew Bible.* Minneapolis: Fortress, 2009.

Burridge, Kenelm. *New Heaven and New Earth: A Study of Millenarian Activities*. Oxford: Blackwell, 1971.

Campenhausen, Hans von. *The Formation of the Christian Bible*. Philadelphia: Fortress, 1972.

Carus, Paul. *The History of the Devil and the Idea of Evil*. New York: Gramercy, 1996.

Chan, Francis, and Preston M. Sprinkle. *Erasing Hell: What God Said about Eternity and the Things We Made Up*. Colorado Springs: Cook, 2011.

Charles, R. H. *The Apocrypha and Pseudepigrapha of the Old Testament*. Oxford: Clarendon, 1913.

Childs, Brevard S. *Myth and Reality in the Old Testament*. Naperville, IL: Allenson, 1960.

Chilton, Bruce. *Abraham's Curse: The Roots of Violence in Judaism, Christianity, and Islam*. New York: Doubleday, 2008.

Clark, Victoria. *Allies for Armageddon: The Rise of Christian Zionism*. New Haven: Yale University Press, 2007.

Collins, John J. *The Apocalyptic Imagination: An Introduction to Jewish Apocalyptic Literature*. Grand Rapids: Eerdmans, 1998.

Cook, Stephen L. *Prophecy & Apocalypticism: The Postexilic Social Setting*. Minneapolis: Fortress, 1995.

Cross, Frank Moore. *Canaanite Myth and Hebrew Epic*. Cambridge: Harvard University Press, 1997.

Crossan, John Dominic. *God and Empire: Jesus against Rome, Then and Now*. New York: HarperOne, 2007.

Danby, Herbert. *The Mishnah*. London: Oxford University Press, 1933.

Dawkins, Richard. *The God Delusion*. New York: Houghton Mifflin, 2006.

Eagleton, Terry. *On Evil*. New Haven: Yale University Press, 2010.

Ehrman, Bart D. *Jesus: Apocalyptic Prophet of the New Millennium*. Oxford: Oxford University Press, 1999.

———. *Lost Christianities: The Battle for Scriptures and Faiths We Never Knew*. Oxford: Oxford University Press, 2003.

———. *Lost Scriptures: Books That Did Not Make It into the New Testament*. Oxford: Oxford University Press, 2003.

Elbert, Jerome W. *Are Souls Real?* Amherst, NY: Prometheus, 2000.

Elliott, Neil. *Liberating Paul: The Justice of God and the Politics of the Apostle*. Minneapolis: Fortress, 2006.

Enns, Peter. *The Evolution of Adam: What the Bible Does and Doesn't Say about Human Origins*. Grand Rapids: Brazos, 2012.

Evans, G. R. *The First Christian Theologians: An Introduction to Theology in the Early Church*. Oxford, UK: Blackwell, 2004.

Ferguson, Everett. *Backgrounds of Early Christianity*. 3rd ed. Grand Rapids: Eerdmans, 2003.

Ferris, Timothy. *The Whole Shebang: A State-of-the-Universe(s) Report*. New York: Simon & Schuster, 1997.

Forbes, Bruce D., and Jeanne H. Kildre. *Rapture, Revelation, and the End Times*. New York: Palgrave Macmillan, 2004.

Friedman, Richard Elliott. *The Bible with Sources Revealed: A New View into the Five Books of Moses*. San Francisco: HarperSanFrancisco, 2003.

Galambush, Julie. *The Reluctant Parting: How the New Testament's Jewish Writers Created a Christian Book*. San Francisco: HarperSanFrancisco, 2005.

# Bibliography

Gehman, Henry Snyder. *The New Westminster Dictionary of the Bible.* Philadelphia: Westminster, 1970.
Grabbe, Lester L. *Judaism from Cyrus to Hadrian.* Vol. 2. *The Roman Period.* Philadelphia: Fortress, 1992.
Graves, Kersey. *The Biography of Satan: Exposing the Origins of the Devil.* Escondido, CA: Book Tree, 1999.
Hamer, Dean H. *The God Gene: How Faith Is Hardwired into Our Genes.* New York: Anchor, 2004.
Hanson, Paul. *The Dawn of Apocalyptic: The Historical and Sociological Roots of Jewish Apocalyptic Eschatology.* Philadelphia: Fortress, 1979.
Herring, George. *Introduction to the History of Christianity.* New York: New York University Press, 2006.
Himmelfarb, Martha. *Tours of Hell: An Apocalyptic Form in Jewish and Christian Literature.* Philadelphia: Fortress, 1983.
Hitchens, Christopher. *God Is Not Great: How Religion Poisons Everything.* New York: Twelve, 2007.
Hobsbawm, Eric. *Bandits.* New York: New Press, 2000.
Horsley, Richard A. *Bandits, Prophets, and Messiahs: Popular Movements in the Time of Jesus.* Harrisburg, PA: Trinity Press International, 1999.
———, ed. *In the Shadow of Empire: Reclaiming the Bible as a History of Faithful Resistance.* Louisville: Westminster John Knox, 2008.
———. *Jesus and Empire: The Kingdom of God and the New World Disorder.* Minneapolis: Fortress, 2003.
———. *Revolt of the Scribes: Resistance and Origins.* Minneapolis: Fortress, 2010.
Jenkins, Philip. *Jesus Wars: How Four Patriarchs, Three Queens, and Two Emperors Decided What Christians Would Believe for the Next 1,500 Years.* New York: HarperOne, 2010.
Johnson, Luke Timothy. *The Gospel of Luke.* Collegeville: Liturgical, 1991.
Josephus, Flavius. *The Works of Josephus.* Translated by William Whiston. Peabody, MA: Hendrickson, 1987.
Käsemann, Ernst. *Commentary on Romans.* Translated and edited by Geoffrey W. Bromiley. Grand Rapids: Eerdmans, 1980.
Kee, Howard Clark, et al. *Cambridge Companion to the Bible.* Cambridge: Cambridge University Press, 1997.
Kelly, Henry Ansgar. *Satan: A Biography.* Cambridge: Cambridge University Press, 2006.
Kelly, J. N. D. *Early Christian Doctrines.* New York: Harper & Row, 1978.
Kirk, G. S. *Myth: Its Meaning in Ancient and Other Cultures.* Berkeley: University of California Press, 1970.
Kloppenborg, John S. *The Earliest Gospel: An Introduction to the Original Stories and Sayings of Jesus.* Louisville: Westminster John Knox, 2008.
Leveson, Jon D. *Creation and the Persistence of Evil: The Jewish Drama of Divine Omnipotence.* Princeton: Princeton University Press, 1988.
Liu, Eric, and Nick Hanauer. *The Gardens of Democracy: A New American Story of Citizenship, the Economy, and the Role of Government.* Seattle: Sasquatch, 2011.
Maxwell-Stuart, P. G. *Satan: A Biography.* Chalford, UK: Amberley, 2008.
McDonald, Lee Martin, and James A. Sanders, eds. *The Canon Debate.* Peabody, MA: Hendrickson, 2002.
McLean, Bethany, and Joe Nocera. *All the Devils Are Here: The Hidden History of the Financial Crisis.* New York: Portfolio/Penguin, 2010.

Mendenhall, George E. *Ancient Israel's Faith and History: An Introduction to the Bible in Context.* Louisville: Westminster John Knox, 2011.

———. *Our Misunderstood Bible.* BookSurge, 2006.

Meyer, Marvin W. *The Gnostic Discoveries: The Impact of the Nag Hammadi Library.* San Francisco: Harper, 2005.

Miller, Robert, ed. *The Apocalyptic Jesus: A Debate.* Santa Rosa, CA: Polebridge, 2001.

Moore, George Foot. *Judaism in the First Centuries of the Christian Era.* Vols. 1 and 2. Cambridge: Harvard University Press, 1950.

Neusner, Jacob. *First-Century Judaism in Crisis:* Eugene, OR: Wipf & Stock, 2006.

———. *From Politics to Piety: The Emergence of Pharisaic Judaism.* Eugene, OR: Wipf & Stock, 2003.

———. *Judaism in the Beginning of Christianity.* Philadelphia: Fortress, 1984.

Nickelsburg, George W. E. *Resurrection, Immortality, and Eternal Life in Intertestamental Judaism and Early Christianity.* Cambridge: Harvard University Press, 2006.

Nickelsburg, George W. E., and James C. VanderKam. *I Enoch.* Minneapolis: Fortress, 2004.

Osterley, W. O. E. *A History of Israel.* Vol. 2. Oxford: Oxford Press, 1932.

Pagels, Elaine. *The Origin of Satan.* New York: Vintage, 1996.

Polkinghorne, John. *God of Hope and the End of the World.* New Haven: Yale University Press, 2002.

Rad, Gerhard von. *Genesis: A Commentary.* London: SCM, 1959.

Ramsay, William M. *The Westminster Guide to the Books of the Bible.* Louisville: Westminster John Knox, 1994.

Randall, Lisa. *Knocking at Heaven's Door: How Physics and Scientific Thinking Illuminate the Universe and the Modern World.* New York: HarperCollins, 2011.

Robinson, James. M. *The Gospel of Jesus: In Search of the Original Good News.* San Francisco: HarperSanFrancisco, 2005.

———. *Jesus: According to the Earliest Witness.* Minneapolis: Fortress, 2007.

Rossing, Barbara R. *The Rapture Exposed: The Message of Hope in the Book of Revelation.* New York: Basic, 2004.

Russell, Jeffrey Burton. *The Devil: Perceptions of Evil from Antiquity to Primitive Christianity.* Ithaca: Cornell University Press, 1977.

Sandell, Michael L. *Justice: What's the Right Thing to Do?* New York: Farrar, Straus & Giroux, 2009.

Sanders, E. P. *Jewish and Christian Self-Definition.* Philadelphia: Fortress, 1980.

Schiffman, Lawrence H. *Reclaiming the Dead Sea Scrolls: The History of Judaism, the Background of Christianity, the Lost Library of Qumran.* Philadelphia: Jewish Publication Society, 1994.

Schroeder, Gerald L. *God according to God: A Physicist Proves We've Been Wrong about God All Along.* New York: HarperOne, 2009.

———. *The Science of God: The Convergence of Scientific and Biblical Wisdom.* New York: Free Press, 1997.

Shermer, Michael. *The Science of Good and Evil: Why People Cheat, Gossip, Care, Share, and Follow the Golden Rule.* New York: Holt, 2004.

Smith, Mark S. *The Early History of God: Yahweh and the Other Deities in Ancient Israel.* Grand Rapids: Eerdmans, 2002.

———. *The Origins of Biblical Monotheism: Israel's Polytheistic Background and the Ugaritic Texts.* New York: Oxford University Press, 2001.

## Bibliography

Soggin, J. Alberto. *Introduction to the Old Testament.* Old Testament Library. Philadelphia: Westminster, 1976.

Stenger, Victor J. *God: The Failed Hypothesis; How Science Shows that God Does Not Exist.* Amherst, NY: Prometheus, 2007.

———. *The New Atheism: Taking a Stand for Science and Reason.* Amherst, NY: Prometheus, 2009.

Tattersall, Ian. *Masters of the Planet: The Search for Our Human Origins.* New York: Palgrave Macmillan, 2012.

Tcherikover, Victor. *Hellenistic Civilization and the Jews.* Jerusalem: Jewish Publication Society, 1959.

Thompson, R. Lowe. *The History of the Devil: The Horned God of the West.* London: Paul, Trench, Trubner, 1929.

Travis, Stephen H. *Christ and the Judgement of God: The Limits of Divine Retribution in New Testament Thought.* Colorado Springs: Hendrickson, 2008.

Waetjen, Herman C. *The Gospel of the Beloved Disciple.* New York: T. & T. Clark, 2005.

———. *The Origin and Destiny of Humanness: An Interpretation of the Gospel According to Matthew.* San Rafael, CA: Crystal, 1976.

———. *A Reordering of Power: A Socio-Political Reading of Mark's Gospel.* Minneapolis: Fortress, 1989.

Westermann, Claus. *Isaiah 40–66: A Commentary.* Old Testament Library. Philadelphia: Westminster, 1969.

Wilson, Edward O. *The Social Conquest of Earth.* New York: Liveright, 2012.

Wink, Walter. *Engaging the Powers: Discernment and Resistance in a World of Domination.* Minneapolis: Fortress, 1992.

———. *Naming the Powers: The Language of Power in the New Testament.* Philadelphia: Fortress, 1984.

———. *Unmasking the Powers: The Invisible Forces That Determine Human Existence.* Philadelphia: Fortress, 1986.

Wolfe, Alan. *Political Evil: What It Is and How to Combat It.* New York: Knopf, 2011.

Wray, T. J., and Gregory Mobley. *The Birth of Satan: Tracing the Devil's Biblical Roots.* New York: Palgrace Macmillan, 2005.

Wright, N. T. *Evil and the Justice of God.* Downers Grove: InterVarsity, 2006.

———. *Judas and the Gospel of Jesus: Have We Missed the Truth about Christianity?* Grand Rapids: Baker, 2006.

———. *Luke for Everyone.* London: SPCK, 2001.

www.ingramcontent.com/pod-product-compliance
Lightning Source LLC
Chambersburg PA
CBHW062043220426
43662CB00010B/1629